HOW TO MASTER THE
BMAT

Unbeatable preparation for success in the BioMedical Admissions Test

Chris Tyreman

KoganPage

LONDON PHILADELPHIA NEW DELHI

While the author has made every effort to ensure that the content of this book is accurate, please note that occasional errors can occur in books of this kind. If you suspect that an error has been made in any of the tests included in this book, please inform the publishers at the address printed below so that it can be corrected at the next reprint.

Publisher's note

Every possible effort has been made to ensure that the information contained in this book is accurate at the time of going to press, and the publishers and authors cannot accept responsibility for any errors or omissions, however caused. No responsibility for loss or damage occasioned to any person acting, or refraining from action, as a result of the material in this publication can be accepted by the editor, the publisher or the author.

First published in Great Britain and the United States in 2009 by Kogan Page Limited
Reprinted 2009, 2010

120 Pentonville Road	525 South 4th Street, #241	4737/23 Ansari Road
London N1 9JN	Philadelphia PA 19147	Daryaganj
United Kingdom	USA	New Delhi 110002
www.koganpage.com		India

© Chris Tyreman, 2009

The right of Chris Tyreman to be identified as the author of this work has been asserted by him in accordance with the Copyright, Designs and Patents Act 1988.

ISBN 978 0 7494 5461 6

British Library Cataloguing-in-Publication Data

A CIP record for this book is available from the British Library.

Library of Congress Cataloging-in-Publication Data
Tyreman, C. J.
    How to master the BMAT : unbeatable preparation for success in the biomedical admissions test / Chris John Tyreman.
        p. ; cm.
    ISBN 978-0-7494-5461-6
    1. Medical colleges--Great Britain--Entrance examinations--Study guides. 2. Medical sciences--Examinations, questions, etc. I. Title.
    [DNLM: 1. Education, Medical--Great Britain--Examination Questions. W 18.2 T992h 2009]
    R772.T97 2009
    610.71'141--dc22

                                        2009022790

Typeset by Saxon Graphics Ltd, Derby
Production managed by Jellyfish
Printed in the UK by CPI Antony Rowe

Contents

Introduction

Use this book to boost your BMAT score

This book will maximize your BioMedical Admissions Test (BMAT) score in the shortest time with the least possible effort. It focuses on the core knowledge in the six key skill areas. There are no chapters dealing with interviews or why you want to be a doctor/vet. Written in a note-taking style, it is easy to pick up and revise without being off-putting due to passages of time-consuming text or wordiness.

Fifty per cent revision, fifty per cent practice

The book is complete in two halves. The first half, of about 100 pages, consists of six sections of revision material for the Maths, Physics, Chemistry and Biology components of the BMAT, with additional notes for problem solving and the writing task. At the end of each section, a set of review questions enables you to identify and improve your weak areas before you sit the test. The second half, also of about 100 pages, consists of practice papers that reflect the BMAT test. Candidates are supported throughout the book, and where possible every question comes complete with its revision topics indicated in brackets; for example (P3b; M6d) means revise Physics topic 3b and Maths topics 6d to answer the question; (B1a; C10b,c) means revise Biology topic 1a and Chemistry topics 10b and 10c.

No other book is required

Do not worry if, for example, you dropped Physics or Chemistry two years ago. With this 'all-in-one book' you can fill in the gaps in your knowledge without having to buy any other books. Even if a subject is new to you, rapid progress is possible because the level of prior knowledge is assumed to be low.

Expanded answers

Some other books provide only a 'right/wrong' marking scheme, which is fine if you have chosen the correct answer but is otherwise of limited help. In this book, almost every question comes with an expanded answer that offers sufficient explanation as to the method involved.

Hints to the solution

It is often the case that a *clue* to the method of answer serves to jog the memory. For this reason, many of the questions include a *hint* as to the solution. Even so, candidates should try to answer the question without referring to the hint (written below the answer choices) in the first instance. For some candidates the hint will 'give the game away', though in many instances it will not and in any case the solution may still be several steps away. This method of learning is an aid to memory and reduces the chances of 'getting stuck' and then having to turn to the answer as the only means forward.

BMAT test format

The Biomedical Admissions Test lasts two hours. It has three sections and the first two are marked by computer. No calculators or dictionaries are permitted.

Section 1: Aptitude and skills: 35 multiple-choice or short-answer questions; time allowed one hour.

Section 2: Scientific knowledge and applications: 27 multiple-choice or short-answer questions; time allowed 30 minutes.

Section 3: Writing task: answer one question from a choice of three; one side of A4 paper; time allowed 30 minutes.

BMAT registration

Entry to the BioMedical Admissions Test is via Cambridge Assessment. Full details of how and where to sit the BMAT are available on the BMAT website: http://www.bmat. org.uk. The test is taken in November and the deadline for standard applications is at the end of September.

A list of universities/courses requiring the BMAT can be found on the UCAS website: http://www.ucas.ac.uk. At the time of writing, the BMAT is taken by students wishing to read medicine, veterinary medicine and related courses at the University of Oxford, the University of Cambridge, Imperial College London, University College London and the Royal Veterinary College.

Part 1

Reviews

1

Aptitude and skills review

A1.   Understanding argument 1: basic aspects
A2.   Understanding argument 2: flaws; types of questions
A3.   Understanding argument 3: example argument
A4.   Critical thinking: Venn diagrams and logic statements
A5.   Shape symmetry
        Aptitude review questions

A1. Understanding argument 1: basic aspects

a) *Argument*

An argument is a short passage of prose that usually contains a *conclusion* and the *evidence* (reasons) supporting it. The evidence is presented in one or more *premises* (statements) that appear plausible within the context of the argument. A conclusion is often expressed at the end of the passage or at the beginning, and its *validity* depends upon: i) the truth of the premises, including any *assumptions* that the reader is expected to take for granted, and ii) the soundness of the reasoning from the evidence to the conclusion.

b) *Conclusion, evidence and assumptions*

i)   **The conclusion** is a judgement based on reasoning from premises; the following words are indicators: therefore, consequently, in summary, so, hence, infer, shows, should, will.

ii) **The evidence** is the knowledge required to support the conclusion; the following words are indicators: obviously, because, for example, in support of, due to, since, as a result of.

iii) **The assumptions** provide the link between the evidence and the conclusion as long as they are true. Assumptions are not stated but are deemed to 'go without saying'; in other words, proof is not given, so you have to read between the lines.

c) *Reasoning*

i) **Deductive:** the conclusion is deduced from generally accepted facts and a minor premise. For example: all planets orbit the sun; Mars is a planet so Mars must orbit the sun.

ii) **Inductive** (most arguments): the conclusion is drawn from minor premises (ie *inferred* from observation and patterns) that are believed to support the general case of something (eg a theory) but do not provide *conclusive* proof; for example, Mars moves around the sun and the earth moves around the sun so the sun is at the centre of all the planets (*probable*). There are three key possibilities: the conclusion is true with true premises and sound (valid) reasoning; the conclusion is false with sound reasoning (but false premises); the conclusion is false with true premises (but unsound reasoning).

A2. Understanding argument 2: flaws; types of questions

a) *Flaws*

These are errors in arguments leading to misleading or unsafe conclusions:

- Confusing correlation with causation. For example, death rates are higher in cancer patients receiving complementary therapies, so complementary therapies must be harmful to health (untrue: patients are seriously ill when orthodox medicine fails).

- Confusion over percentages and numbers. For example, 15 per cent of road fatalities involve motorbikes and 75 per cent involve cars so it is five times safer to ride a motorbike than to drive a car (untrue: fewer than one in 50 vehicles are motorbikes).

- Over-generalizing. For example, nine out of 10 people interviewed said they would buy a small car next time so there is little market for the large car (sample too small or unrepresentative; all those interviewed drove small cars).

- Logical fallacy: the premises are true but do not support the conclusion (though it may be true). For example, if A follows B (true) then so must C, D and E (false). Note that a true conclusion can be arrived at (accidentally) with false premises.

b) *Question types*

Questions in the BMAT take various forms:

■ A short paragraph that contains a conclusion and the evidence that supports it. You should assume that the evidence (premises) is true for the purposes of the argument; ie, do not introduce your own knowledge base or opinions. Choose an answer that:

- is the *best conclusion* (ie the main thrust of the argument or what can be safely *inferred*), or
- identifies what has been *implied* (not directly stated or assumed, but suggested or hinted at), or
- identifies what *must be assumed* for the conclusion to hold true, or
- would *weaken* the argument if it were true (ie contradictory statement; alternative explanation), or
- would *strengthen* the argument if it were true (ie supportive statement; consistent), or
- would show the conclusion to be untrue (eg a *fallacy*).

Read every answer choice before selecting the best response.

■ A longer passage of more than one paragraph followed by three questions designed to check reading comprehension; numerical data may be included.

A3. Understanding argument 3: example argument

Argument: Motorway speed limits should be increased to 80 mph. The current limit of 70 mph was introduced in 1965 when cars were less well engineered than today. Modern cars are designed for speeds well in excess of 80 mph so there is no need to restrict motorway speeds to 70 mph.

Conclusion: Motorway speed limits should be increased to 80 mph.
Evidence (taken as fact): Modern cars are better engineered.
Evidence (taken as fact): They are designed for speeds well over 80 mph.
Assumption (can be challenged): Driving at 80 mph is safe if the car is designed to do it.

The above argument can be weakened by contradictory evidence or strengthened by supportive evidence. For example:

■ *Significantly weakening*: It may be the case that motor vehicle accidents on motorways usually involve speeds in excess of the current limit (challenges a questionable assumption).

■ *Significantly strengthening*: It may be the case that most accidents are not caused by speeding (supports 70 mph+).

■ *Slightly weakening*: It may be the case that higher speeds lead to more serious accidents (true but outside scope of argument).

■ *Slightly strengthening:* It may be the case that there have been major improvements in highway engineering since 1965 (true but outside scope of argument).

■ *Inference*: Increasing the motorway speed limit to 80 mph will not lead to more accidents (main thrust of argument).

■ *Irrelevant:* Carbon dioxide emissions will increase if the speed limit is raised (true but outside scope of argument).

A4. Critical thinking: Venn diagrams and logic statements

a) *Venn diagrams*

For example: 48 patients attend a chest clinic; 29 have asthma (A), 30 have bronchitis (B) and 8 have neither disease. How many patients have both asthma and bronchitis? Method: draw a rectangle (*universal set*) containing two overlapping circles A and B.

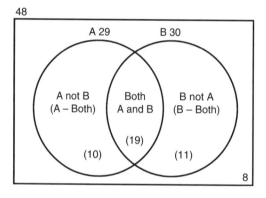

(A not B) + Both = 29; (B not A) + Both = 30; add to give:

1) (A not B) + (B not A) + 2 × Both = 59
2) (A not B) + (B not A) + Both = 48 – 8 = 40

1) – 2) gives Both = 19

Summary: A only = 10; B only = 11;
both A and B = 19; A + B + Both = 40; neither = 8;

b) *Logic statements*

Logic statements are two premises that lead to a conclusion. For example:

1. All cattle are animals.
2. All bulls are cattle.
3. Therefore all bulls are animals.

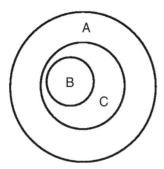

(NB: this is a logic statement diagram, not a Venn diagram)

A5. Shape symmetry

a) *Reflection symmetry*

Reflection symmetry is also known as line symmetry; it occurs where a shape appears identical, or symmetrical, either side of a line, as in a mirror image. Shapes can have one, two or more lines of symmetry, for example:

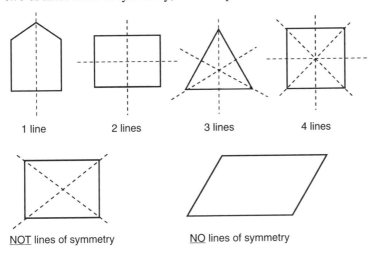

1 line   2 lines   3 lines   4 lines

NOT lines of symmetry   NO lines of symmetry

b) *Rotational symmetry*

A shape has rotational symmetry if it can be rotated about its centre and still look the same. A square has four orders of rotational symmetry (90°, 180°, 270°, 360°).

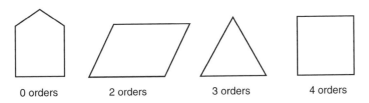

0 orders   2 orders   3 orders   4 orders

Aptitude review questions

Q1. (A2, 3) The nuclear industry claims that its power stations are safe and no threat to people. If this is true, then why do they locate their power plants away from population centres? By doing so they are admitting that nuclear power is potentially dangerous to local communities.

Which one of the following, if true, would most seriously weaken the above argument?

A. Reactors are located away from communities as part of a general risk management strategy.
B. The potential for harm following any leak is significantly reduced.
C. Cooling water for the reactors is not available in populated areas.
D. Costs are lower and local communities are less likely to oppose planning applications.

Answer [   ]

Q2. (A2, 3) Bio-diesel is not an alternative to petroleum-based diesel in the fight against carbon dioxide emissions from car exhausts; carbon is carbon and when it burns it produces carbon dioxide. The source of the carbon does not influence the size of the carbon footprint.

Which one of the following, if true, would significantly weaken the above argument?

A. Bio-fuel crops fix carbon dioxide during photosynthesis.
B. Bio-diesel accounts for less than 5 per cent of diesel combusted.
C. Cars are not the major source of carbon dioxide emissions.
D. Carbon-dioxide-fixing rainforest is cut down to make way for bio-diesel crops.

Answer [   ]

Q3.	(A2, 3) Clinically obese patients, ie those with a Body Mass Index (BMI) of more than 30, should be denied knee-joint surgery. The risk of complications following surgery is too great and the new joint is more likely to fail under the load.

Which two of the following, if true, would most weaken the above argument?

A.	Joint life is only reduced in the morbidly obese (BMI > 40).
B.	Clinically obese patients are entitled to treatment just any much as anyone else.
C.	Obesity is a significant risk factor for osteoarthritis.
D.	General health is more important than clinical obesity where complications are concerned.
E.	It would be better if clinically obese patients were made to lose weight before they underwent joint surgery.

Answer ☐

Q4.	(A2, 3) ACE-inhibitors, beta-blockers, calcium-channel blockers and diuretics are the four main classes of drugs used to lower high blood pressure. However, in a randomized controlled trial (RCT) drinking beetroot juice was found to be equally effective in reducing blood pressure. These findings offer an alternative method of controlling hypertension.

Which two of the following, if true, would seriously weaken the above argument?

A.	The participants consumed a large volume of beetroot juice.
B.	Beetroot juice is an effective diuretic.
C.	The control group drank water.
D.	None of the participants had high blood pressure.
E.	Reducing dietary salt and eating more green leafy vegetables also helps to reduce high blood pressure.

Answer ☐

Q5. (A2, 3) Building offshore wind turbines on a massive scale is not the best way to cut carbon emissions. The money saved by not building them could be directed towards energy efficiency savings in the home. Some council properties have been supplied with free, energy-saving incandescent light-bulbs. These use 80 per cent less electricity, producing 25 kg less carbon dioxide per year. Supplying every household with three incandescent bulbs will save more energy than the UK's target for energy to be supplied by wind power.

Statement: Traditional light-bulbs are an obsolete technology and should be phased out, but the UK needs a diverse range of modern technologies to combat climate change.

Which of the following best describes how the short statement relates to the argument?

A. It refutes the argument entirely.
B. It lends qualified support for the argument.
C. It summarizes the main point of the argument.
D. It neither supports nor refutes the argument.
E. It is largely irrelevant to the main points of the argument.

Answer [ ]

Q6. Place the following four sentences in the order in which they form the most coherent passage.

A. Originally, being politically correct meant avoiding ideas or language that might offend minority groups.
B. Not infrequently this viewpoint is enforced by a politically correct majority that has not even consulted the minority it purports to support.
C. Political correctness has steadily chipped away at our freedom of speech.
D. More recently it has been seen as tolerating only one viewpoint that is deemed to be acceptable or true.

Answer [ ]

2

Maths review

M1. Mental arithmetic review 1: basic operations

Calculators are not allowed in the BMAT, so memorize the mental arithmetic table.

	1	2	3	4	5	6	7	8	9
1	1	2	3	4	5	6	7	8	9
2	2	4	6	8	10	12	14	16	18
3	3	6	9	12	15	18	21	24	27
4	4	8	12	16	20	24	28	32	36
5	5	10	15	20	25	30	35	40	45
6	6	12	18	24	30	36	42	48	54
7	7	14	21	28	35	42	49	56	63
8	8	16	24	32	40	48	56	64	72
9	9	18	27	36	45	54	63	72	81

For the purposes of the BMAT, mental arithmetic means with a pen and paper, so write down as many steps as you need to in a calculation to minimize the chance of making a careless mistake. All you want is the correct answers; impressive mental arithmetic counts for very little. Use 'place values':

Example: $7532 + 4316 = 7 + 4(\times 1000) + 5 + 3(\times 100) + 3 + 1(\times 10) + 8$

Write down $= 11\,000 + 800 + 48$

Similarly: $7532 \times 3 = 21\,000 + 1500 + 90 + 6 = 22\,500 + 96 = 22\,596$

Division: $456 \div 12 = (480 \div 12) - (24 \div 12) = 40 - 2 = 38$

The following rules are helpful when dividing:

i) If the last digit is 0, 2, 4, 6 or 8, the number will divide by 2.

ii) If the last digit ends in 0 or 5, the number will divide by 5.

ii) If the last digit ends in 0, the number will divide by 10.

ii) If the last two digits divide by 4, the number will divide by 4.

Factorize large numbers (useful for cancelling fractions) by dividing them by prime numbers (2, 3, 5, 7, 11, 13 etc). Example: $504 = 2 \times 2 \times 2 \times 3 \times 3 \times 7$.

M2. Mental arithmetic review 2: further operations

a) *Negative numbers*

Addition: $(-2) + 6 = 4$; $2 + (-6) = -4$; $(-2) + (-6) = -8$.
Subtraction: $(-2) - 6 = -8$; $2 - (-6) = 8$; $(-2) - (-6) = 4$.
Multiplication: $2 \times (-6) = -12$; $(-2) \times 6 = -12$; $(-2) \times (-6) = 12$.
Division $6 \div (-3) = -2$; $(-6) \div 3 = -2$; $(-6) \div (-3) = 2$.

b) *BIDMAS = Order of working out problems (first to last)*

B = Brackets.
I = Indices.
D = Division.
M = Multiplication.
A = Addition.
S = Subtraction.

Example: $(35 + 15) \times 2^2 + 10 \times 14 - 480 \div 3$

Work from left to right obeying the BIDMAS rules:

$50 \times 4 + 140 - 160 = 200 - 20 = 180$

c) *Index laws*

i) **examples of using indices (with powers of 10):**
$10^5 \times 10^2 = 10^7$; $10^5 \div 10^2 = 10^3$; $(10^3)^2 = 10^6$; $10^{-6} = 1/10^6$;
$10^{1/2} \times 10^{1/2} = 10^1 = 10$ (ie $10^{1/2} = \sqrt{10}$); $10^0 = 1$.

ii) **surds:** eg $\sqrt{12} = \sqrt{4} \times \sqrt{3} = 2\sqrt{3}$; $\sqrt{10} \div \sqrt{5} = \sqrt{10/5} = \sqrt{2}$.

iii) **logarithm:** if $x = b^y$ then $\log_b x = y$ by definition; examples are: $100 = 10^2$ then $\log_{10} 100$ $= 2$ (log to the base 10 of $100 = 2$); $32 = 2^5$ then $\log_2 32 = 5$ (log to the base 2 of $32 = 5$); also note that $\log_b x + \log_b y = \log_b (xy)$ so $\log_b 100 + \log_b 100000$; $= 2 + 6 = \log_b (10^8)$; in other words, add log values when multiplying numbers and subtract log values when dividing numbers.

d) *Factors*

Factors divide into other numbers exactly without leaving a remainder. For instance, the factors of 24 are: 1 and 24, 2 and 12, 3 and 8, 4 and 6 (ie 1, 2, 3, 4, 6, 8, 12 and 24); the factors of 15 are: 1 and 15, 3 and 5 (ie 1, 3, 5 and 15). The highest *common factor* (HCF) of 24 and 15 is 3. Factors are used for breaking down large numbers and for cancelling fractions.

e) *Progressions (trends)*

i) **Arithmetic series:** consecutive numbers increase or decrease in value by the *common difference* (*d*), eg 6, 9, 12, 15, 18, $d = 3$; for an initial value of *a* the formula is: $a + (a + d) + (a + 2d)\ldots n^{th}$ term $= (a + (n - 1)d)$; eg 25th term is $6 + 24 \times 3 = 78$; sum of series $S_n = n \times (\text{first} + \text{last})/2$

ii) **Geometric series:** consecutive numbers increase or decrease in value by a constant factor known as the *common ratio* (*r*) eg 4, 20, 100, 500, 2500; common ratio $r = 5$; the formula is $a + ar^2 + ar^3 + ar^4 + ar^5$ and the nth term is ar^{n-1}; for instance, in the above series the 8th term is 4×5^7; sum of series $S_n = a \times (r^n - 1)/(r - 1)$.

iii) **letters** may be used in place of numbers; for example A = 1, B = 2, C = 3, D = 4 etc.

M3. Fractions 1: basic arithmetic

a) *Fractions*

Fractions: cancel (simplify) fractions by dividing the numerator and the denominator by the same *prime factors* (2, 3, 5, 7, 11, 13 etc), starting with the smallest (2) to give the *equivalent fractions*. Example:

eg $\dfrac{72}{180} = \dfrac{36}{90} = \dfrac{18}{45} = \dfrac{6}{15} = \dfrac{2}{5}$ (divide by 2, 2, 3, and 3)

i) **Addition/subtraction of fractions:** if the denominators are the same, write the denominator once and add/subtract the two top numbers.

eg $\dfrac{5}{7} + \dfrac{3}{7} = \dfrac{8}{7} = 1\dfrac{1}{7}$ If the denominators are different, find a common denominator that both denominators will divide into.

eg $\dfrac{5}{6} + \dfrac{3}{8}$ The most obvious common denominator is 48 (6 × 8). However, the lowest common denominator (LCD) is 24. It makes the working out easier and can be found by comparing equivalent fractions.

ii) **Multiplication/division of fractions:** for multiplication, multiply the two numerators together and the two denominators together.

eg $\dfrac{5}{6} \times \dfrac{7}{10} = \dfrac{5 \times 7}{6 \times 10} = \dfrac{35}{60} = \dfrac{7}{12}$; alternatively you can cross-cancel the 5 and 10

as a first step: $\dfrac{1}{6} \times \dfrac{7}{2}$ and then multiply.

iii) **Division:** similar to multiplication except that the fraction on the right-hand side is turned upside down and then multiplied by the fraction on the left-hand side.

eg $\dfrac{5}{6} \div \dfrac{7}{10}$ becomes $\dfrac{5}{6} \times \dfrac{10}{7}$; cancelling 6 and 10 by 2 gives

$\dfrac{5}{3} \times \dfrac{5}{7} = \dfrac{25}{21} = 1\dfrac{4}{21}$ (1 whole $= \dfrac{21}{21}$)

M4. Fractions 2: improper fractions; ratios

a) *Improper fractions*

Improper fractions (numerator greater than the denominator) are added, subtracted, multiplied and divided in exactly the same way as for proper fractions. The answer shown below is a *mixed number* containing both a whole number and a fraction.

eg $\dfrac{7}{4} - \dfrac{1}{8} = \dfrac{14}{8} - \dfrac{1}{8} = \dfrac{13}{8} = 1\dfrac{5}{8}$

Mixed numbers are added and subtracted by keeping the whole numbers and the fractions separate, and multiplied and divided by converting to improper fractions.

eg $1\dfrac{1}{8} \times 2\dfrac{3}{4} + 1\dfrac{7}{8} = \dfrac{9}{8} \times \dfrac{11}{4} + 1\dfrac{7}{8} = \dfrac{99}{32} + 1\dfrac{7}{8} = 3\dfrac{3}{32} + 1\dfrac{7}{8} = 3\dfrac{3}{32} + 1\dfrac{28}{32} = 4\dfrac{31}{32}$

b) *Ratios*

Ratios are similar to fractions with the whole divided into parts. Example: divide 80 in the ratio 3:1.

1st step: work out the number of parts in the whole, in this case: 3 + 1 = 4 (four quarters).
2nd step: work out the proportional parts (the fractions); these are 3⁄4 and 1⁄4.
3rd step: multiply the whole by the proportional parts: 3⁄4 × 80 = 60; 1⁄4 × 80 = 20 (check: 60 + 20 = 80).

Ratios can be simplified in the same way as fractions by cancelling both sides by a common factor (by 2, 3 etc).
Example: The ratio of boys to girls in a class of 36 is 20:16. Express this ratio in its simplest terms.
20:16 = 10:8 = 5:4 (five boys for every four girls).

M5. Decimals 1: fraction/decimal conversions and basic arithmetic

a) *Fractions to decimals and vice versa*

i) **Fraction to decimal:** re-write as a division; eg 3/25 re-write as 25 into 3.00.

$$\begin{array}{r} 0.12 \\ \hline 25 \,|\, 3.00 \end{array}$$

ie

ii) **Decimal to fraction:** use place values; eg 0.6 = 6 tenths = 6/10 = 3/5; 0.004 = 4 thousandths = 4/1000 = 1/250.

Equivalent fractions of the more common decimals:
eg 0.25 = one-quarter; 0.5 = one-half; 0.75 = three-quarters.
0.1 = one-tenth; 0.2 = one-fifth; 0.125 = one-eighth; 0.375 = three-eighths.
0.01 = one-hundredth; 0.005 = five-thousandths.

b) *Basic arithmetic*

i) **Addition and subtraction:** maintain place values:
eg 0.5 + 0.043 + 0.00021 = 0.54321.

ii) **Multiplication:** for multiples (powers) of 10 the decimal point is moved to the right by the respective number of zeros.
eg 0.95 × 10 = 9.5   0.95 × 100 = 95   0.95 × 1000 = 950.

For numbers other than 10 you ignore the decimal point and then add it back in using the following rule:

Decimal places in the question = decimal places in the answer.

For example 8 × 10.75, ignore the decimal point:
8 × 1075 = 8 × 1000 + 8 × 75 = 8000 + 4 × 150 = 8600.
Number of decimal places = 2; ie 8600 becomes 86.00.
(NB check magnitude: 8 × 10.75 is approximately 8 × 11 = 88.)

iii) **division:** reverse of multiplication for multiples (powers) of 10: move the decimal point to the left.

40.75 ÷ 10 = 4.075; ÷ 100 = 0.4075; ÷ 1000 = 0.04075.
Division of or by decimal numbers can be facilitated by using a multiplication step to make the division easier or by using powers of 10 to remove or move the decimal point.
eg 65 ÷ 0.25 = 65 × 4 ÷ 1 = 260.
eg 65.25 ÷ 5 = 130.5 ÷ 10 = 13.05.

M6. Decimals 2: rounding (decimal place, significant figure) and standard form

a) *Decimal place*

For example, multiply 1.725 by 5 and give your answer to two decimal places (2 dp). Answer: $1.725 \times 5 = 8.625 = 8.63$ to 2 dp. Method: if the *number to the right* of the decimal place you are rounding to is 5 *or above*, then you increase the number in the decimal place by one; if is less than 5 it remains the same. So $4.8573 = 4.857$ to 3 dp, 4.86 to 2 dp, 4.9 to 1 dp, 5.0 to 0 dp; rounding to 0 dp = rounding to the nearest whole number:

12.49 to the nearest whole number is 12 (round down);
12.50 to the nearest whole number is 13 (round up).

b) *Significant figures*

For example, multiply 1.725 by 5 and give your answer to two significant figures (2 sf). Answer: $1.725 \times 5 = 8.625 = 8.6$ to 2 sf. Method: similar to decimal place in that you look at the number to the right of the significant figure you are rounding to, but start from the *left-most non-zero term* (not from the decimal point). So $4.8573 = 4.857$ to 4 sf, 4.86 to 3 sf, 4.9 to 2 sf and 5.0 to 1 sf.

Any number can be rounded using significant figures: for example, $125\,890 = 130\,000$ to 2 sf; $0.003759 = 0.0038$ to 2 sf (leading zeros are not significant). Significant figures and decimal place may or not be the same, for example: 2.916 is 2.92 to 2 dp and 2 sf; $0.02916 = 0.03$ to 2 dp, but 0.029 to 2 sf.

c) *Standard form (scientific notation)*

For example, $125\,890$ in standard form is 1.25890×10^5. Method: use powers of 10 so that only one digit comes in front of the decimal point. The following show correct and incorrect use:

$37\,500 = 3.75 \times 10^4$ in standard form.
$37\,500 = 375 \times 10^2$ true but this is not in standard form.
$0.00249 = 2.49 \times 10^{-3}$ in standard form.
$0.00249 = 0.249 \times 10^{-2}$ true but this is not in standard form.
$37\,500.00249 = 3.750000249 \times 10^4$ in standard form.
With rounding $= 3.75000025 \times 10^4$ to 9 sf; 3.7500×10^4 to 5 sf.
3.750×10^4 to 4 sf; 3.75×10^4 to 3 sf; 3.8×10^4 to 2 sf.

M7. Per cent (%)

a) *Percentages*

Percentages can be expressed as fractions with denominators of 100 or as decimals by moving the decimal point of the numerator two places to the left.

eg $75\% = \dfrac{75}{100} = \dfrac{15}{20} = \dfrac{3}{4}$ or $\dfrac{75.0}{100} = 0.75$

To work out a percentage figure you multiply by the percent expressed either as a fraction or as a decimal; eg 30 per cent of 120:

$\dfrac{30}{100} = \dfrac{3}{10}$; $\dfrac{3}{10} \times 120 = 3 \times 12 = 36$ or

$30\% = 30 \div 100 = 0.3; 0.3 \times 120 = 3 \times 12 = 36.$

To convert any number to a percent, multiply it by 100%:

For example, $0.3 = 0.3 \times 100 = 30\%; 1.5 \times 100 = 150\%; 1/5 \times 100 = 20\%.$

Alternatively, to convert a less obvious fraction to a percent (or a decimal), express the denominator as a factor of 100.

eg $\dfrac{11}{25} = \dfrac{11 \times 4}{25 \times 4} = \dfrac{44}{100} = 0.44 = 44\%$

b) *Percentage change*

Percentage change $= \dfrac{\text{change in value}}{\text{original value}} \times 100\%$

Example: a car accelerates from 40 mph to 60 mph. What is the percentage increase in speed?

$\dfrac{60 - 40}{40} \times 100\% = \dfrac{20}{40} \times 100\% = 0.5 \times 100\% = 50\%$ increase

Example: A car brakes from 60 mph to 40 mph. What is the percentage decrease in speed?

$\dfrac{60 - 40}{60} \times 100\% = \dfrac{20}{60} \times 100\% = \dfrac{1}{3} \times 100\% = 33.3\%$ decrease

Use the original or initial value as the denominator with change.

M8. Time and clocks

a) *Analogue/digital clocks*

Analogue/digital clocks convert from the 12-hour clock to the 24-hour clock by re-writing the time as a four-digit number and adding 12 hours to all pm times.

For example: 8.30 am = 08:30 (oh eight-thirty hours).
10.55 pm = 10.55 + 12 hrs = 22:55 (twenty-two fifty-five hours).

Fractional parts of an hour are converted to minutes by multiplying the fraction (or its decimal) by 60 minutes:
1/4 hr = 0.25 × 60 = 15 min; 1/10 hr = 0.1 × 60 = 6 min.

You can add or subtract times as follows:
15:45 + 1 hr 50 min = 15:45 + 2 hr – 10 min = 17:35.
21:35 – 55 min = 21:35 – 1 hr + 5 min = 20:40.

Candidates should recognize the following conversions:

1 week (7 days) = 168 hours; 1 day (24 hours) = 1440 minutes.
1 hour (60 minutes) = 3600 seconds. Leap year (÷ 4) = 366 days.
eg 1.5 hr ÷ 5 = 0.3 hrs = 0.3 × 60 min = 3 × 6 min = 18 min.
eg 1 hr ÷ 100 = 1 × 60 × 60 ÷ 100 = 1 × 6 × 6 = 36 sec.

b) *Clock hands questions*

Wear a wrist watch if it helps!
Hour-hand rotation = 360° ÷ 12 hours = 30° per hour.
Minute-hand rotation = 360° ÷ 60 minutes = 6° per minute.
Angle between the hands: 90° at 15:00 and 21:00; 180° at 18:00.

i) **For all times when the minute hand points exactly to an hour** the angle between the hands is approximately given by:

(hr shown by hour hand – hr shown by minute hand) × 30°

and precisely by the figure given in i) plus min ÷ 60 × 30°, ie min ÷ 2° (the extra distance moved by the hour hand for the fraction of the hr).
For example, at 08:20 the angle between the hands is approx (8–4) × 30° = 120° and exactly 120° + 20 ÷ 2° = 130° (the hour hand has moved on an additional 1/3 hr (10°) in 20 minutes).

ii) **For all times when the minute hand does not point to a full hour** it can be shown that the angle between the hands is given by:

$(30° \times hr - 6° \times min) + min \div 2°$

For example, at 08:25 the angle between the hands = $(30° \times 8 - 6° \times 25) + 12.5° = 90° + 12.5° = 102.5°$ exactly.

M9. Areas, perimeters, volumes and surface area

a) *Areas*

- Square of side length $a = a \times a = a^2$.
- Rectangle/parallelogram: base $(b) \times$ height $(h) = b \times h$.
- Triangle: 1/2 base $\times$ vertical height = $1/2\ bh$.
- Trapezium: 'half the sum of the parallel sides $\times$ distance between them': ie $\frac{1}{2}(a + b)d$.
- Circle of radius r, diameter D: πr^2 (pi r squared) or as $D = 2r$: $\pi D^2/4$.
- Sector of a circle: $\pi D^2/4 \times$ sector angle $\div 360$.
- Cylinder of base radius r and height h: $\pi r^2 h$; sphere: $4\pi r^2$.
- Border = area of outer shape – area of inner shape.

b) *Perimeters*

The perimeter is the distance all the way around the outside of the shape. Examples are: square = 4 $\times$ length of side; rectangle = 2 $\times$ length $\times$ breadth; circumference of a circle C = $2\pi r = \pi D$; perimeter of a sector = $(\pi D \times$ sector angle $\div 360) + r + r$.

c) *Volumes of solids*

- Cube of side length $a = a \times a \times a = a^3$.
- For any uniform prism: area of cross-section $\times$ the length (or base $\times$ height $\times$ length).
- For a sphere: $4/3\ \pi r^3$.
- For a cone or pyramid: 1/3 area of base $\times$ height.

d) *Surface area*

This is total amount of exposed area.

- Cube = $6a^2$.
- Rectangular prism, base b, length l, height h: $2(bh + lh + bl)$.
- Hollow cylinder: circumference $\times$ height = $2\pi rh$.
- Solid cylinder: $2\pi rh + 2(\pi r^2)$.

e) *Ratios of lengths, areas and volumes*

For similar shapes, if the ratio of the side lengths is $a:b$ ('a to b') then the ratio of the areas is $a^2:b^2$ and the ratio of the volumes is $a^3:b^3$. For example, for two cubes of side lengths 4 cm and 2 cm respectively the ratio of side lengths is 4:2 = 2, the ratio of the face areas is then $2^2 = 4$ and the ratio of the volumes is $2^3 = 8$ (check: 64 cm^3:8 cm^3).

M10. Algebra 1: substitution and re-arranging

a) *Substitution*

Letters are used in place of numbers (constants) to describe the 'general case' of something; x and y (variables) are the most common letters used in algebra. For example, substitute $x = 6$ and $y = 9$ in $x^2 - 3y + 3$; $36 - 27 + 3 = 12$.

b) *Expanding brackets*

i) **Any 'term' outside a bracket** multiplies each of the terms inside the bracket, moving from left to right: $5(y - 3z) = 5 \times y + 5 \times -3z = 5y - 15z$. Similarly: $-2y(7 - 4x + z) = -14y + 8xy - 2yz$.

ii) **Pair of brackets, four terms:** $(a + b)(c + d) = ac + bc + ad + bd$ (multiply everything in the second brackets by everything in the first: 'FOIL': Firsts (ac), Insides (bc), Outsides (ad), Lasts (bd)).

c) *Re-arranging*

Terms containing the letter you want are moved to one side of the equation (eg the left-hand side).

i) **Linear equations:** eg $x = y + z$ can be re-arranged to make y the subject by subtracting z from both sides of the equation: *leaves y on its own*: $x - z = y + z - z$ giving $x - z = y$; ie $y = x - z$.

For example, find x if $4x + y = z$:
Step 1: subtract y from both sides to give $4x + y - y = z - y$ so $4x = z - y$;
Step 2: divide both sides by 4.

$$\frac{4x}{4} = \frac{z - y}{4} \text{ then } x = \frac{z - y}{4}$$

Examples of linear equations (formulae) are temperature conversions (°C to °F) and electricity charges; for example, to convert temperature from °F to °C: $F = 9/5 \ C + 32$.

To make °C the subject:

Step 1: subtract 32 from both sides to give: $F - 32 = 9/5\,C + 0$.
Step 2: multiply both sides by 5/9 to give $5/9(F - 32) = 5/9 \times 9/5\,C$; $5/9\,(F - 32) = 1 \times C$, ie $C = 5/9\,(F - 32)$.

ii) **Equations with fractions:** eg $y = \dfrac{x+3}{5} - \dfrac{x}{2}$; multiply by the lowest common denominator (LCD = 10) to remove the fractions, giving $10y = 2(x + 3) - 5x$, before expanding the brackets and collecting like terms: $10y = 6 - 3x$. If the denominators contain variables you can multiply them to find a common denominator.

iii) **Equations with square-root signs:** square both sides if the letter you want is inside the square-root sign.

M11. Algebra 2: simultaneous and quadratic equations

a) *Factorizing*

This is the reverse of expanding the brackets (M10b).

i) **'Difference of two squares':** $x^2 - y^2 = (x + y)(x - y)$;
$16a^2 - 9b^2 = (4a)^2 - (3b)^2 = (4a + 3b)(4a - 3b)$.

ii) **'Trinomial':** $x^2 + bx + c$ factorize by finding two numbers that when added together equal b and multiplied together equal c. For example, $x^2 + 5x + 6$; $(x\ \ )(x\ \ )$; find a pair of factors of 6 (1 and 6; 2 and 3 are the choices) that when multiplied give $+6$ and when added give $+5$, ie 2 and 3: $(x + 2)(x + 3)$.

Example: $x^2 - x - 12$; $(x\ \ )(x\ \ )$; find a pair of factors of -12 that when multiplied give -12 and when added give -1 (use trial and error on factors 1, 2, 3, 4, 6, 12 (one $+$, the other $-$) to find the solutions 3 and -4, ie $(x + 3)(x - 4)$.

In a 'perfect square' the b-term is twice the size of that inside the bracket.
For example, $x^2 + 10x + 25 = (x + 5)^2$; solve $x^2 + 6x + 2 = 0$; $(x + 3)^2 - 7 = 0$; $x + 3 = \sqrt{7}$, giving $x = -3 +/- \sqrt{7}$

b) *Simultaneous equations*

Expand brackets; collect x and y terms on the left-hand side; multiply by factors to make coefficients of one term equal (eg y) then add or subtract to eliminate one term (y) and solve for the other (x).
For example, 1) $5x = 3y + 33$; 2) $3(4x - y) = 12 - 7y$; solve for x and y:

Expand brackets and collect x and y terms on the left-hand side:
1) $5x - 3y = 33$;
2) $12x + 4y = 12$.

Make the coefficients of y the same in each equation, as follows:
1) $\times 4$ gives $20x - 12y = 132$; 2) $\times 3$ gives $36x + 12y = 36$.

Add 1) and 2): $56x = 168$ so $x = 3$; $x = 3$ in 1) gives $3y = 15 - 33$, so $y = -6$.

c) Quadratic equations: $x^2 + bx + c = 0$

i) **Solve with factors** (see also a) ii above) eg $x^2 - 6x + 5 = 0$;
$(x\quad)(x\quad)$; $(x - 5)(x - 1)$; so either $x - 5 = 0$ or $x - 1 = 0$, giving $x = 5$ or 1 as the solutions for x ('the roots').

ii) **For 'non-factorizing' quadratic equations** solve for a, b and c in the expression $ax^2 + bx + c = 0$ using the general solution:

$$x = \frac{-b \pm \sqrt{b^2 - 4ac}}{2a}$$

Using the coefficients (a, b, c) from $x^2 - 6x + 5 = 0$ gives $a = 1$, $b = -6$ and $c = 5$; so $x = (6 \pm \sqrt{36 - 20}) \div 2$; therefore $x = (6 + \sqrt{16}) \div 2$ or $x = (6 - \sqrt{16}) \div 2$; giving $x = (10) \div 2$ or $x = (2) \div 2$; ie $x = 5$ or 1 as before (example only; use if there are no obvious factors).

M12. Averages: mean, median, mode; weighted

a) Averages

i)   Mean: the total of the numbers divided by the number of numbers.

ii) Median: the middle number in a group of numbers that have been ranked in numerical order from lowest to highest.

iii) Mode: the value that occurs most frequently.

For example, the weights in kilograms of seven students were as follows:
60 kg, 73 kg, 66 kg, 69 kg, 57 kg, 60 kg, 71 kg.

i)   Mean = 456 kg $\div$ 7 = 65.1 kg.

ii) Median: 57, 60, 60, **66**, 69, 71, 73; the middle number is 66.

If there is an even number of numbers then there is no 'middle value' as such, so you need to calculate the mean of the two middle numbers. To find the middle of a large group of numbers you add 1 to the number of numbers (n) and divide by 2; ie $(n + 1) \div 2$. Take for example 100 numbers: $(n + 1) \div 2 = (100 + 1) \div 2 = 50.5$ so the median is the mean of the 50th and 51st numbers.

iii) Mode = 60 because it occurs the most frequently (twice). If two values occur with equal frequency then the group is bi-modal. If more than two numbers are equally popular then the mode is not used for expressing the average value.

iv) Range = maximum minus the minimum: $73 - 60 = 13$ kg.

b) *Weighted average*

Some exam results count more than others towards the final result, as with university degree classifications. Example: a ratio of 1:3 for the 4th-year marks to the 5th-year marks; ie 4th year = 25 per cent; 5th year = 75 per cent. Overall percentage is given by Yr4 × 25 per cent + Yr5 × 75 per cent. Suppose that a student scores 120 out of 200 in year 4 and 240 out of 300 in Year 5. If the tests are weighted 25 per cent for Year 4 and 75 per cent for Year 5, what is the overall percentage mark?

Yr 4: $120/200 \times 100\% = 60\%$; Yr 5: $240/300 \times 100\% = 80\%$.
Now apply the weighting: overall $\% = 60 \times 25\% + 80 \times 75\% = 15 + 60 = 75\%$.

General case: **multiply each percentage mark by its percentage weight and add the results together.**

M13. Pie and bar charts, line and scatter graphs, tables

a) *Pie charts*

These display the relative sizes of component parts. Full circle (360°) = 100% of the data; 180° = one-half (50%), 120° = one-third (33.3%), 90° = one-quarter (25%). Each degree = 1/360th of the total quantity. Multiplying the total by the fraction/percentage gives the number for the sector. Always check for a key or subheading, especially with twin charts.

b) *Bar charts (graphs)*

These compare different categories of data, for example A-level subjects, or school results in different years. The bars can be drawn vertically or horizontally and the height (or length) of each bar corresponds to the size of the data. In stacked (compound) bar charts the bars are split into two or more lengths that represent different data sets, making it easier to compare the data than when bars are placed side by side. In a histogram the data are grouped into class intervals along the x-axis, for example 10–19, 20–29, 30–39 and so on, to show the distribution of the data; the data intervals are continuous so the bars must touch. NB the *area* of the bar represents the size of the data (bars can be wider or narrower depending on the class interval, eg age 40–59 is twice as wide as 30–39).

c) *Line graphs*

The data (displayed in a table) are plotted as a series of points joined by straight lines. The controlling quantity (eg time) is plotted on the x-axis and the quantity it controls (eg distance travelled) is plotted on the y-axis. In multiple line graphs, two or more lines are shown together on the same axes to facilitate comparisons, for example results in physics, chemistry and biology A levels. The gradient (m) of a straight line can be found by choosing two convenient points on the line, then $y = mx + c$ where gradient (m) = change in y ÷ change in x, and c is the value of y where the line intercepts the y-axis ($x = 0$).

d) *Scatter graphs*

These look similar to line graphs without the line, in other words with the plotted points only. Sometimes a 'line of best fit' is drawn through all of the points (not point to point). This 'regression line' can be judged by eye (and extrapolated) or it can be calculated. The line identifies the extent of any relationship (*correlation*) between the x and y values. In a strong correlation the points lie close to a straight line; x and y increase (*positive correlation*) or decrease (*negative correlation*) in proportion to each other. In a weak correlation the points are not close to the line; a state of no correlation exists if the points appear to be randomly distributed (no line can be drawn).

e) *Tables*

Read along a column and down a row to locate the data; most tables will have several columns and several rows. Data in a table may be reflected in a chart.

M14. Cumulative frequency, box and whisker plots

a) *Cumulative frequency graphs*

These are 'S'-shaped graphs showing, for example, how many candidates achieved a particular mark and below. The running total of frequencies (not the actual frequency) is plotted against the data values.

i) **Median:** the x value of the middle data value (eg marks score) located halfway up the cumulative frequency curve (axis), ie 50% cumulative frequency (50th percentile). Half of the data fall below the x-value at this point on the curve and half lie above it. Percentiles divide the data into 100 equal parts.

ii) **Upper quartile** (75th percentile): three-quarters of the data fall below the x-value at this point on the curve and one-quarter of the data are above it (ie it shows where the top 25% lie).

iii) **Lower quartile** (25th percentile): one-quarter of the data fall below the x-value at this point on the curve and three-quarters of the data are above it (ie it shows where the bottom 25% lie).

iv) **Inter-quartile range** (75th percentile minus 25th percentile): shows where the middle 50% of the data lie.

b) *Box and whisker plots*

These are derived from cumulative frequency graphs and display several key pieces of statistical information. Two boxes and two whiskers split the data into four quarters, as shown in the figure below.

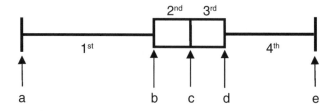

a: the lowest data value (end of whisker);
b: the lower quartile at the 25th percentile;
c: the median at the 50th percentile;
d: the upper quartile at the 75th percentile;
e: highest value (end of whisker);
d–b: the inter-quartile range (half the results lie here);
e–a: the range (end of one whisker to the end of the other).

M15. Geometry 1: angles and lines, triangles, other shapes

a) *Angles and lines*

i) Where two lines intersect, the opposite angles are equal.

ii) Where a line intersects two parallel lines the corresponding angles are equal; the interior alternate angles are equal; the exterior alternate angles are equal.

iii) Angles on a straight line add up to 180°.

iv) Angles around a point add up to 360°.

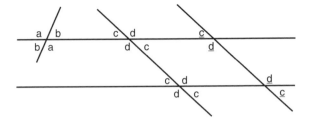

a + b = 180°; c + d = 180°; c + d + c + d = 360°; exterior alternate angles (c̲) are equal; interior alternate angles (d̲) are equal.

b) *Triangles*

i)   The three interior angles of any triangle add up to 180°.

ii) Scalene: all three sides are of different length.

ii) Equilateral: all sides are of equal length; all angles are equal to 60°.

iii) Isosceles: opposite sides of equal length and two angles equal.

iv) Right angle: one angle is 90°.

c) *Other shapes*

i) **For any regular quadrilateral** (square, rectangle, parallelogram, rhombus, trapezium, kite) and irregular quadrilaterals (any four-sided shape other than those described above): the four interior angles add up to 360°.

ii) **For any shape with *n* sides:** the sum of the interior angles is given by $(180n - 360)°$, ie $180(n - 2)°$; for a regular polygon having all sides the same length (eg pentagon, hexagon, heptagon, octagon) each interior angle equals $180(n - 2)° \div n$.
For example, in a regular octagon: each interior angle = $180(8 - 2)° \div 8 = 1080 \div 8 = 135°$.

M16. Geometry 2: Pythagoras and trigonometric functions

a) *Pythagoras' theorem for any right-angled triangle*

Opposite² + adjacent² = hypotenuse² (longest side).

In other words, if you know the length of two sides you can use Pythagoras to find the third side. The six smallest Pythagorean triples (sides with whole numbers) are (3,4,5), (5,12,13), (6,8,10), (9,12,15), (8,15,17), (7,24,25); for instance, $3^2 + 4^2 = 5^2$ (ie a 3,4,5 triangle). Four of the above triples are primitives and two are non-primitives (6,8,10), (9,12,15). All Pythagorean triples are *multiples* of one of the primitives, for example (3,4,5) × 2 = (6,8,10); × 3 = (9,12,15); × 4 = (12,16,20); (7,24,25) × 2 = (14,48,50).

b) *Sin, cosine and tan: (angle depends on ratio of side lengths)*

i) Right-angled triangles:
sin = opposite ÷ hypotenuse; cos = adjacent ÷ hypotenuse
tan = opposite ÷ adjacent. 'SOH...CAH...TOA'.
eg for a 6,8,10 triangle we have:

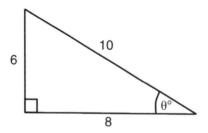

sin θ = 6/10 = 0.6; cos θ = 8/10 = 0.8; tan θ = 6/8 = 0.75.
Inverse functions θ = sin⁻¹ 0.6 = cos⁻¹ 0.8 = tan⁻¹ 0.75.

ii) **Non-right-angled triangles:** when a is the side opposite angle A, b is the side opposite angle B and c is opposite angle C then (when three pieces of data are known).
Sine law: a ÷ sin A = b ÷ sin B = c ÷ sin C (used when at least one angle and its opposite side are known (eg A and a), plus one more side or one more angle.
Cosine law: $a^2 = b^2 + c^2 - 2bc \cos A$ (used when all three side-lengths are known or two sides and the angle between them).

iii) **Angles greater than 90°**, sin x = sin (180 − x); −cos x = cos (180 − x);
for example, x = 120°; sin 120 = sin 60; −cos 120 = cos 60.
Sine wave: graph of y = sin x; amplitude = 1 (y-axis), period (x-axis) = 360° (2π);
for example, graph of y = 10 sin x; amplitude = 10, period = 360° (2π); sine is negative for angles between 180° and 360° wave goes below the x-axis.
Cosine wave: same as sine wave only shifted to the left by 90° (π/2); cos is negative for angles between 90° and 270°; wave goes below the x-axis.

M17. Circle theorems

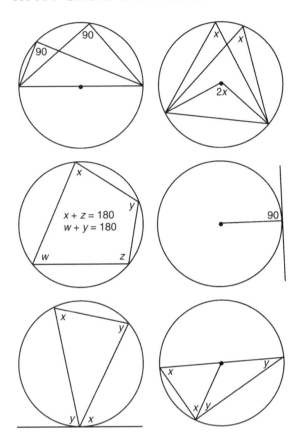

M18. Inequalities

a) *Linear inequalities*

For example:

i) **Solve** $x - 6 < 0$ (x minus 6 is less than 0); add 6 to both sides to give $x < 6$.

ii) **Solve** $-x^2 + 9 < 0$; subtract 9 from both sides to give:
$-x^2 < -9$ then *multiply both sides by −1 and reverse the inequality sign* ie $x^2 > 9$ so $x > 3$.

iii) **Solve** $5x - 12 > 8$ ($5x$ minus 12 is greater than 8); add 12 to both sides to give: $5x > 20$ so $x > 4$.

iv) **Solve** $4 - 3x < 10$; subtract 4 from both sides to give $-3x < 6$;
divide both sides by −3 and reverse the inequality sign: $x > -2$.

v) **Find the range** for x in $-4 < 3x + 5 < 11$; subtract 5 from all three parts to give $-9 < 3x < 6$; dividing by 3 gives $-3 < x < 2$.

vi) **Solve** $8 - 2x \leq 5$ (8 minus $2x$ is less than or equal to 5); subtract 8 from both sides to give $-2x \leq -3$ then multiply both sides by -1 and reverse the sign to give $2x \geq 3$ so $x \geq 1.5$.

b) *Quadratic inequalities*

For example: find the range of values of x for which $x^2 - 8x < -12$; add 12 to both sides: $x^2 - 8x + 12 < 0$ then treat as a normal quadratic: $x^2 - 7x + 12 = 0$ to get the roots, ie $(x - 2)(x - 6)$, so $x = 2$ or 6.

    To find the range of values for $x^2 - 8x + 12 < 0$, graph the data for $x^2 - 7x + 12 = y$ and find the range of x values for which $y < 0$. Draw the graph from $y = 0$ when $x = 2$ or 6; $y = 12$ when $x = 0$, $(x^2 - 8x + 12 = y)$; quadratic equations form parabolic/U-shaped curves.

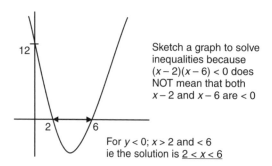

Sketch a graph to solve inequalities because $(x - 2)(x - 6) < 0$ does NOT mean that both $x - 2$ and $x - 6$ are < 0

For $y < 0$; $x > 2$ and < 6 ie the solution is $2 < x < 6$

M19. Probability 1: basic concepts

a) *Defining probability (P)*

P values range from 0 to 1 and can be written as a decimal, percentage, fractions or ratio:

$0 = 0\%$ = impossible.
$0.1 = 10\%$ certainty, 1/10 or 1 in 10 chance (1:10).
$0.25 = 25\%$ certainty, 1/4 or 1 in 4 chance (1:4).
$0.5 = 50\%$ certainty, 1/2 or 1 in 2 chance (1:2).
$0.75 = 75\%$ certainty, 3/4 or 3 in 4 chance (3:4).
$1 = 100\%$ certainty.

Also: 50% certainty = 50% uncertainty ('fifty-fifty').
Similarly: 40% certainty = 60% uncertainty ('forty-sixty').

b) *Equation*

Probability of a given event E, $P(E)$ is given by:

$P(E)$ = number of times E occurs ÷ total number of outcomes.

c) *The 'and' rule and the 'or' rule.*

For independent events:

i) Probability (P) of A *and* B = $P(A) \times P(B)$; that is to say, the probability of both equals the product of the individual probabilities. For example, find the probability of throwing a 3 *and* a 4 on a dice with two successive throws: $P(A \text{ and } B) = P(A) P(B) = 1/6 \times 1/6 = 1/36$.

ii) Probability (P) of A *or* B = $P(A) + P(B)$.
For example, find the probability of throwing a 6 *or* a 4 on a dice: $P(A \text{ or } B) = P(A) + P(B) = 1/6 + 1/6 = 2/6 = 1/3$

For dependent events:

iii) $P(A \text{ and } B) = P(A) P(B \text{ after } A)$.
For example, find the probability of drawing an ace from a 52-card pack, then drawing a second ace without putting the first one back:
$P(A \text{ and } B) = P(A) P(B \text{ after } A) = 4/52 \times 3/51 = 1/13 \times 1/17$.
For example, find the probability of drawing a black card *or* a king from a 52–card pack:
$P(A \text{ or } B) = P(A) + P(B) - P(A \text{ and } B)$.
$P(A \text{ or } B) = 26/52 + 2/52 - (26/52 \times 2/52) = 28/52 - 1/52 = 27/52$.
(26 black cards and 2 black kings, ie not mutually exclusive.)

For mutually exclusive events:
iv) $P(A \text{ and } B) = P(A) \times P(B) = 0$; $P(A \text{ or } B) = P(A) + P(B) = 1$; eg tossing a coin: probability of a head and tail together = 0; probability of a head or a tail = 1.

M20. Probability 2: tree diagrams

a) *Rules*

The total of the probabilities on two branches from a single point = 1; probabilities add vertically and multiply horizontally from branch to branch.

Example: A car manufacturer buys 80% (0.8) of its widgets from Firm A and the remainder from Firm B. Two % of the widgets from Firm A are defective and 5% of the widgets from Firm B are defective. If one widget is withdrawn from a mixed bag of widgets, find the probability that:

i)   The widget will be defective and made by Firm A.

ii) The widget will be defective and made by Firm B.

iii) The widget will be defective and made by either firm.

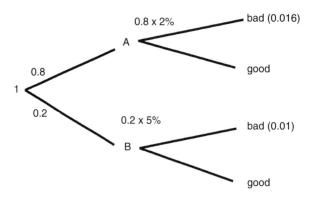

i) 0.016 (1.6%); ii) 0.01 (1%); iii) 0.016 + 0.01 = 0.026 (2.6%).

Example: 10 000 people are tested for a drug. Of these, 1% are drug users and the rest are not. For drug users there is a 1% chance of a false negative and for non-drug users there is a 1% chance of a false positive. What is the probability that a person chosen at random who tests positive is actually a drug user?

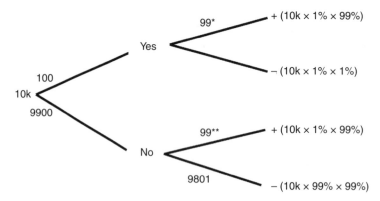

Probability $E = 99* \div (99* + 99**) = 99 \div 198 = 50$ per cent.

M21. Permutations and combinations

a) *Counting principle*

For example, a car is available in eight different colours, four engine sizes and three levels of trim = 8 × 4 × 3 = 96 choices.

b) *Permutations*

i) **Permutations for a set $n = n!$ (ie n factorial)**
(factorial 10 = 10 × 9 × 8 × 7 × 6 × 5 × 4 × 3 × 2 × 1).
For example, permutations of a three-letter group, A,B,C, are as follows:

ABC, ACB, BAC, BCA, CAB, CBA (the order of selection is important);
ie Permutation $P = 6 = 3 × 2 × 1$ (ie 3 factorial; 3!);

For a four-letter group A,B,C,D; $P = 4! = 4 × 3 × 2 × 1 = 24$.

ii) **Permutations of r objects from a set $n = n! ÷ (n − r)!$**
For example, the number of possible permutations of any two-letter group chosen from a group of 10 letters A,B,C,D,E,F,G,H,I,J is given by: $P = 10 ÷ (10 − 2)! = 10! ÷ 8! = 10 × 9 = 90$.

c) *Combinations*

i) **Combination for objects from a set $n = n! ÷ (n − k)!k!$**
For example, the number of possible combinations of any two-letter group chosen from a group of 10 letters A,B,C,D,E,F,G,H,I,J (the order of selection is not important) is given by:

$C = 10! ÷ (10 − 2)!2! = 10! ÷ 8!2! = 10 × 9 ÷ 2! = 45$ possible ways of choosing two letters from 10.

d) *Combinations vs permutations*

Example: in eight-ball pool there are eight balls numbered from 1 to 8. These are placed in a sack and three balls are drawn out at random. i) How many different combinations of three balls are possible? ii) How many different permutations of three balls are possible?

i) $C = 8! ÷ (8 − 3)!3! = 8! ÷ 5!3! = 8 × 7 × 6 ÷ 3 × 2 = 56$.
ii) $P = 8! ÷ (8 − 3) = 8! ÷ 5! = 8 × 7 × 6 = 336$.

For example, balls 1, 2 and 3 = one combination of balls with six possible permutations (1,2,3; 1,3,2; 2,1,3; 2,3,1; 3,1,2; 3,2,1 or 3!)

Maths review questions

Q1.   (M9) If the area of the square in the figure below is 4 cm², what is the area of the shaded region?

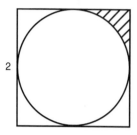

A. $4 - \pi$
B. $2 - \pi$
C. $1 - 0.5\pi$
D. $1 - 0.25\pi$
E. 0.75π

Answer [ ]

Q2.   (M16) What is the area of the square?

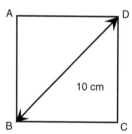

A. 100 cm²
B. $\sqrt{200}$ cm²
C. $\sqrt{50}$ cm²
D. $\sqrt{150}$ cm²
E. 50 cm²

Answer: [ ]

Q3.   (M9, 16) ABC is an equilateral triangle of side x. What is its area?

A. $x^2(3/4)$
B. $\sqrt{3}(x^2/4)$
C. $2x(\sqrt{3})$
D. $10\sqrt{3}$
E. $3x/4$

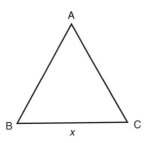

(hint: split base in two)

Answer [   ]

Q4. (M16) What is the length of h in the triangle shown below?

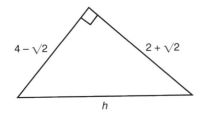

A. $2\sqrt{(6-\sqrt{2})}$
B. $6(4-\sqrt{2})$
C. $6\sqrt{2}$
D. $2(6-\sqrt{2})$
E. $2\sqrt{(4-\sqrt{2})}$

Answer [   ]

Q5. (M15) The area of the shape ABCD is 60 cm². What is its perimeter?

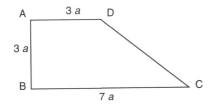

A. 30 cm
B. 32 cm
C. 34 cm
D. 36 cm
E. 38 cm

Answer [   ]

Q6. (M17) What is the length of the arc AB if the circle has a diameter of 10 cm?

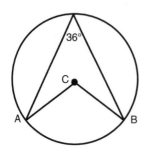

    A. 2π cm
    B. 3π cm
    C. 4π cm
    E. 6π cm

(hint: circle theorem)

Answer

Q7. (M2) Calculate $[6^{2/3}]^6 + [10^{4/5}]^5$.

    A. 1.75×10^{11}
    B. 1.296×10^8
    C. 1.1296×10^4
    D. 1.6×10^5

Answer

Q8. (M2) Calculate $\dfrac{9 \times 2^{15} - 6 \times 8^5}{3 \times 8^5}$

Answer

Q9. (M10, 11) Find x if $(5x - 2)^2 = 4$.

Answer

Q10. (M10, 11) If $(2x)^8 = (2x + 3)^4$, what is one possible value of x?
    A. 1/4
    B. 1/3
    C. 4/3
    D. 3/2

Answer

Q11. (M10, 11) A purse contains £5.70 in a mixture of 50p and 20p coins. If there are 15 coins in total, how many of these are 20p coins?

Answer ____

Q12. (M9, 11) Cubes A, B and C fit snugly into cube D. The volume of cube A is eight times that cube B and the volume of cube C is one-eighth that of cube B. If the volume of cube D is 1000 cm³, what is the side-length of cube A?

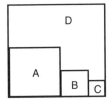

   A. $2\frac{2}{9}$
   B. $5\frac{5}{7}$
   C. $4\frac{6}{7}$
   D. $6\frac{3}{7}$

Answer ____

Q13. (M11) In a quadratic equation, the sum of the roots is 0 and the product of the roots is –16. What is the equation?

   A. $x^2 + 8 = 0$
   B. $x^2 - 8 = 0$
   C. $x^2 + 16 = 0$
   D. $x^2 - 16 = 0$

Answer ____

Q14. (M19ciii) You are dealt two cards from a shuffled pack of 52 playing cards. What is the probability that the first card will be a spade and the second card will be a spade?

   A. 1:15
   B. 1:16
   C. 1:17
   D. 1:18

Answer ____

Q15. (M18) Solve the inequality $x(2x + 6) \leq 8$.

    A. $x = 1; x = -4$
    B. $x \leq 1; x \leq -4$
    C. $4 \leq x \leq -1$
    D. $-4 \leq x \leq 1$

Answer ☐

Q16. (M10) If $a = \dfrac{y - b}{y - c}$, express y in terms of a and b.

    A. $(ac - b)/(a - 1)$
    B. $(a - 1)/(ac - b)$
    C. $(b - ac)/(a - 1)$
    D. $(ac + b)/(a - 1)$

Answer ☐

Q17. (M16biii) If a cosine graph is $90°$ out of phase with the sine graph shown below, and the cosine of $0° = 1$, which of the following statements must be true?

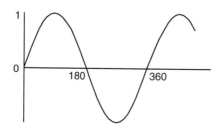

    A. $\sin 90 = \cos 180$
    B. $\sin 0 = \cos 180$
    C. $\sin 180 = \cos 360$
    D. $\sin 90 = -\cos 90$
    E. $\sin 270 = \cos 180$

(hint: draw cos)

Answer ☐

Physics review

P1. Measurements and prefixes

a) *The SI system*

There are seven base units in the SI system: length in metres (m), mass in kilograms (kg), time in seconds (s), electric current in amperes (A), temperature in kelvins (K), luminous intensity in candelas (cd) and amount of substance in moles (mol). The remaining SI units are derived from combinations of these base units. For example:

joules (J) = kg m^2 s^{-2};
volts (V) = kg m^2 s^{-3} A^{-1}.

Base units help to reveal links between derived units; in the above examples the kg m^2 terms can be cancelled to give:

J/V = A s, so J = V A s;
and ampere second = coulomb (C).
Thus J = V C (joules = volts × coulombs)

b) *SI prefixes*

The following SI prefixes describe orders of magnitude ranging from 10^{-12} to 10^{+12} and most are in steps of 1000.

Factor	Name	Symbol	Example
10^{-12}	pico	p	picofarad (pF)
10^{-9}	nano	n	nanometre (nm)
10^{-6}	micro	μ	microgram (μg)
10^{-3}	milli	m	milligram (mg)
10^{-2}	centi	c	centimetre (cm)
10^{-1}	deci	d	decilitre (dl)
10^{+3}	kilo	k	kilonewton (kN)
10^{+6}	mega	M	megapascal (MPa)
10^{+9}	giga	G	gigajoule (GJ)
10^{+12}	tera	T	terawatts (TW)

P2. Conventions for units, symbols and numbers

Use the following conventions when writing SI units, symbols and numbers:

a) Choose units that limit the use of decimals, fractions or numbers greater than 1000. For example, use 500 micrograms NOT 0.5 mg; 1.5 mg NOT 1500 micrograms; avoid Greek letters and write out microgram in full (on prescriptions) to avoid confusion with mg.

b) Leave a space between the number and the unit and avoid plurals (s); for example, 25 mg NOT 25mg or 25 mgs; 2.5 L NOT 2.5L.

c) With the exception of the litre (L), the symbols for units should be in lower-case letters unless the unit is named after an individual. For example, metre (m); second (s); kilometre (km); but volts (V); newtons (N); watts (W); joules (J); kelvins (K)

d) A forward slash or a negative exponent can be used to separate the top unit from any unit it is divided by, but use only exponents if more than one slash is required. For example, g/cm^3 or $g\ cm^{-3}$; m/s^2 or $m\ s^{-2}$ but for clarity $kg/m/s^2$ should be written as $kg\ m^{-1}\ s^{-2}$

e) Use gaps to break up large numbers into groups of three digits; a comma is non-standard because it is a decimal separator in some European countries. No gap is required with four-digit numbers, though you may use one if you wish.
For example, 1 275 000; 1,275,000 is non-standard (but frequently used);
0.259 75 NOT 0.259,75;
5002 (or 5 002) but NOT 5,002.

f) Do not use a multiplication sign between units; use a space or a raised dot. For example, newton metre: N m (or N·m), NOT N × m.

P3. SI base units for length, volume, mass

a) *Length*

1 metre (m) = 100 centimetres (cm).
1 kilometre (km) = 1000 metres (m).
1 centimetre = 10 mm (mm).
1 mm = 1000 micrometres (1000 microns (non-SI)).
1 micrometre (μm) = 0.001 mm = 0.000 001 metres (10^{-6} m).
1 nanometre = 10^{-9} m (and 1 ångström (non-SI) = 0.1 nanometre).

b) *Mass*

1 kilogram (kg) = 1000 grams (g).
1 gram (g) = 1000 milligrams (mg).
1 milligram (mg) = 1000 micrograms.
1 metric ton (t) = 1000 kg = 1 megagram (Mg).

c) *Volume*

1 litre (L or l) = 1000 millilitres (mL).
1 decilitre (dL) = 0.1 L = 100 mL.
1 centilitre (cL) = 0.01 l = 10 mL.
1 millilitre (mL) = 0.001 litre.
1 ml = 1 cm^3 and 1 L = 1000 cm^3.
1 microlitre (μL) = 0.001 mL = 0.000 001 l (10^{-6} mL) .

1 cubic metre (m^3) = 1000 L.
1 cubic decimetre (dm^3) = 1 litre.

d) *Density*

Density (ρ) = mass per unit volume (g cm^{-3} or kg m^{-3}); 1 g cm^{-3} = 1000 kg m^{-3}.
Relative density (specific gravity) = density relative to water (no units). The density of water can be taken as 1 g cm^{-3} (= 1 kg L^{-3} = 1 t m^{-3}).

P4. Equations of motion

a)   Speed is a scalar quantity measured in metres per second.
    Average speed = distance ÷ time taken (m s^{-1}); distance = speed × time.

b)   Velocity is a vector; it measures speed in a given direction.
    Average velocity = net displacement ÷ time taken (m s^{-1}).
    Zero net displacement = zero average velocity.
    For example, a car travels 10 km north and then 10 km south at an average speed of 50 kilometres per hour. Net displacement = 0 (10 and –10); average velocity = 0. (NB distance travelled = 20 km; displacement = 0 km.)
    With uniform (constant) velocity the magnitude of the speed and the direction of motion remain constant.

c)   Acceleration is a vector that measures change in velocity per second; the units are metres per second per second (ie metres per second squared (m s^{-2})).
    acceleration (a) = change in velocity (v in m s^{-1}) ÷ time taken (× s^{-1})
    = $(v - u)/t$ (final velocity v; initial velocity u)
    = v/t (when $u = 0$, ie 'from a standing start').

d)   There are three more equations that describe motion under uniform (constant) acceleration:
    $v = u + at$;
    $v^2 = u^2 + 2as$;
    $s = ut + 1/2at^2$;
    where s = distance travelled in time t.

e)   In circular motion the direction is continually changing so acceleration is taking place; this *centripetal acceleration* is towards the centre of the circle and is given by: $a = v^2/r$ (where r = radius); for one revolution, distance = circumference = $2\pi r$ so $2\pi r = vT$ (distance = velocity × time) and $T = 2\pi r/v$ (where T = time for one revolution, or the 'period').

P5. Graphs of motion

a) *Distance versus time graphs*

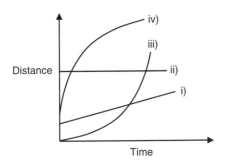

i)   Constant velocity: *slope of the line = velocity.*

ii) Zero velocity (stationary/at rest; no slope).

iii) Increasing velocity = positive acceleration (becoming steeper).

iv) Decreasing velocity = negative acceleration (becoming less steep), for example, when braking and coming to a halt (line eventually horizontal).

b) *Velocity versus time graphs*

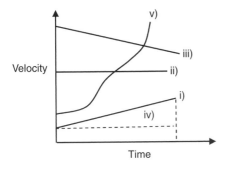

i)   Increasing velocity = *slope of line = uniform (constant) acceleration.*

ii) Uniform velocity = constant speed.

iii) Decreasing velocity = uniform deceleration.

iv) Distance travelled = area under the graph (triangle + rectangle).

v)   Non-uniform velocity (count full and half squares to calculate area).

P6. Projectile motion

a) Substitute g (acceleration due to gravity) for a, and h (height) for s in the equations of motion:

$v = u + gt$ $v^2 = u^2 + 2gh$ $h = ut + 1/2gt^2$.

b) Time: for an object thrown vertically upwards, the time to reach the highest point (u known) is given by $v = u + at$ and $v = 0$ at the highest point so $0 = u - gt$, giving $t = u/g$. The object takes the same amount of time to return to the ground and arrives at the same speed that it left, so total flight time $= 2u/g$.

c) Height: for an object dropped vertically from a cliff or down a well (t known, $u = 0$), calculate the height (h) from $h = 1/2gt^2$ or $5gt^2$ (take $g = -10$ m s^{-2}).

d) Height: for an object thrown vertically upwards from the ground (u known), calculate the maximum height (h) from $v^2 = u^2 + 2gh$ with $v = 0$ at the highest point, so $h = u^2/2g$ or $u^2/20$ ($g = -10$ m s^{-2}; deceleration).

e) Range: for an object thrown horizontally from a cliff known, treat the horizontal motion (x-direction) and the vertical motion (y-direction) separately. Calculate the range (x) from $x = vt$ where v is the horizontal velocity, and t is the time in flight; t can be calculated from the drop height: $h = 1/2 \ gt^2$ so $t = \sqrt{(2h/g)}$.

f) (Unlikely to be tested) For projectiles fired at an angle of θ to the horizontal, the maximum range (x) occurs when $\theta = 45°$; then the height and range;

h is given by: $(u^2 \sin^2\theta)/2g$ ie $u^2/4g$ at 45° (half that of h at 90°);

x is given by $(u^2 \sin 2\theta)/g$ ie u^2/g at 45° (twice h at 90°).

For example, a projectile is fired vertically and reaches a height of 2000 m.

b) Time to the highest point given by: $h = 0.5gt^2$; $t = \sqrt{(2h/g)}$.

$t = \sqrt{(4000/g)} = \sqrt{(400} = 20$ s; time of flight 20 s × 2 = 40 s.

b) Initial velocity: from $t = u/g$, $u = tg = 200$ m s^{-1}.

f) Fired at 45° to the horizontal the projectile would achieve a height of 1000 m and a range of 4000 m (ignoring air resistance).

P7. Force and motion (Newton)

a) Newton's first law: a body remains stationary or in uniform motion unless acted on by a force (such as friction).

b) Newton's second law: a force causes an acceleration: $F = ma$ where F is in newtons, m in kilograms and a in m s^{-2}; a force of one newton gives an acceleration of one metre per second squared to a mass of one kilogram.

c) Acceleration due to gravity is 9.81 m s^{-2} or ≈ 10 m s^{-2} so the force on a mass of 1 kg, experienced as weight (W), is:

$W = mg \approx 1 \times 10$ N ie 1 kg weight ≈ 10 N (downwards).

d) Circular motion: the acceleration towards the centre is given by $a = v^2/r$ and since $F = ma$ then $F = mv^2/r$ where r = radius of the circle.

e) Newton's third law: action and reaction are equal; that is to say, forces come in pairs. Weight, for example, is supported by a force *normal* (perpendicular) to the surface.

f) Friction force (tangential) necessary for an object to slide by overcoming friction is proportional to the normal force and the coefficient of friction (μ). Friction force = $\mu \times$ normal force.

g) Terminal velocity in free fall is governed by Newton's second law; it is reached when the downward force due to gravity (the weight) is balanced by the upward friction force due to air resistance (the drag); with no net force the acceleration ceases.

Net force F_{net} = Weight (W) – Drag (D).

$W - D = 0$ or $W = D$ at the terminal velocity.

The drag increases with speed and frontal area. Heavier objects reach higher terminal velocities than lighter objects of similar shape because there is more weight 'left over' after the drag.

P8. Force, work, power and energy

a) Work done in joules (J) by a force in newtons (N) moving a distance in metres (m) is given by:

work done (J) = force × distance (N m).

Thus one joule is the work done when a force of one newton moves through a distance of one metre.

b) Power is the rate of doing work and is measured in watts (W).

Power (W) = work done ÷ time taken (J s^{-1}).

Thus one watt is the power required to move a force of one newton through a distance of one metre in one second.

For someone of mass m (kg) to run upstairs climbing a height h (metres) in time t (s), the power required is given by:

Power (W) = force × distance ÷ time taken = mgh/t;

= force × velocity = mgv.

c) Energy is the capacity to do work, and like work done, it is measured in joules. The law of conservation of energy states that energy can neither be created nor destroyed, only changed from one form to another; energy–mass equivalence: $E = mc^2$.

Kinetic energy (KE) is the energy of motion.

Potential energy (PE) is stored energy: gravitational potential energy, chemical potential energy and elastic potential energy.

KE = $1/2\ mv^2$ and PE = mgh.

For falling bodies (or bodies thrown upwards) energy is conserved, so we have: PE lost = KE gained (or if up, PE gained = KE lost).

Thus $mgh = 1/2\ mv^2$ or $1/2\ mv^2 + mgh$ = constant.

Note: PE gained or lost depends on changes in vertical height and _not on speed and path_.

P9. Universal gravitation, satellites and escape velocity

a) Newton's law of universal gravitation states that every object in the universe attracts every other object with a force that is proportional to the product of their masses $(m_1 m_2)$ and inversely proportional to the square of separation (r^2) from centre to centre.

Thus $F = \dfrac{G\, m^1\, m^2}{r^2}$ where G is the universal gravitational constant.

On earth the force on an object of mass m is given by $F = mg$.

Thus $mg = \dfrac{G\, mM}{r^2}$ so $g = \dfrac{G\, M}{r^2}$ (earth of mass M, radius r).

Note that the gravitational force exerted by the earth on a body equals the gravitational force exerted by the body on the earth.

b) On leaving the surface of the earth, gravity decreases in inverse proportion to the square of the distance from the earth's centre. For a satellite of mass m orbiting the earth in uniform circular motion, $F = mv^2/r$ (r = distance of satellite from the earth's centre).

Thus $\dfrac{G\, mM}{r^2} = \dfrac{mv^2}{r}$ giving $v^2 = \dfrac{GM}{r}$ and $v = \sqrt{\dfrac{GM}{r}}$

c) For an object to escape the earth's gravitational field it must leave the surface with sufficient kinetic energy to overcome the force of gravity, at which point all its kinetic energy $(1/2\ mv^2)$ will have been converted to potential energy (mgr).

Thus $1/2\ mv^2 = mgr = \dfrac{G\, mM}{r}$ giving $v^2 = \dfrac{2GM}{r}$ so $v = \sqrt{\dfrac{2GM}{r}}$

The escape velocity (v) is the speed that an unpowered rocket must be launched at to overcome the earth's gravity (neglecting air resistance); powered rockets can leave the earth's gravitational field at any speed.

You are unlikely to be tested on the formula but you could be given one to re-arrange.

P10. Force, momentum and impulse

a) Momentum of a moving object is the product of its mass and its velocity:
Momentum (p) = mass (m) × velocity (v) = mv;
and $F = ma$; $v = u + at$; ie $a = (v - u)/t$ so $F = m(v - u)/t$.
Thus Force = change in momentum ÷ time taken;
or Force × time = change in momentum = impulse.

b) Two objects collide (m_1 and m_2): the action and reaction forces are equal (Newton's third law) and as the contact times are the same, so are the changes in momentum. In other words, total momentum before collision = total momentum after it.

c) Elastic collision (snooker balls): both the momentum and the kinetic energy are conserved:

conservation of momentum: $m_1u_1 + m_2u_2 = m_1v_1 + m_2v_2$;

conservation of KE: $1/2(m_1u_1^2 + m_2u_2^2) = 1/2(m_1v_1^2 + m_2v_2^2)$.

d) Inelastic collision (car crash): the momentum is conserved but some of the kinetic energy is lost as heat. A typical collision involves one stationary object ($u_2 = 0$) and both objects sticking together after collision ($v_2 = v_1$), thus:

conservation of momentum with m_2 stationary before impact and both objects linked after the collision: $m_1u_1 = (m_1 + m_2)v_2$;

loss of kinetic energy: $1/2\, m_1u_1^2 > 1/2(m_1 + m_2)v_2^2$.

e) Momentum is a vector. If two objects are moving towards each other then motion to the right should be signed as positive and motion to the left as negative ($m_1u_1 + m_2(-u_2)$). If elastic, the relative velocity before collision = relative velocity after collision: $V_1 - V_2 = U_2 - U_1$ (*signed vectors*); for example m_1 travelling east at 4 m s^{-1} with m_2 travelling west at 6 m s^{-1}: $U_2 - U_1 = -6 - (+4) = -10$ m s^{-1} ($= V_1 - V_2$).

P11. Force, stress and strain

a) Material under load (eg a suspension bridge cable): the stress is given by:

Stress = force ÷ area (N m^{-2} or pascals Pa); the units are the same as for pressure.

The strain is given by:

Strain = extension ÷ length (no units).

For a given material:

Stress ÷ strain = constant = Young's modulus of material.

Thus the strain is proportional to the stress up to the elastic limit (Hooke's law). Beyond the limit of proportionality (elastic limit) the material only partially springs back when the load is removed, leaving it permanently stretched (plastic deformation).

b) Hooke's law for springs: the force exerted by a spring in tension is proportional to the distance (x) it is stretched (up to the elastic limit).

Force = $-kx$ where k is the spring constant (N m^{-1}).

Thus for a spring stretched to double its natural length, the return force will be half that of a spring stretched to four times its natural length. The work done in stretching (or compressing) a spring is equal to the product of the average force and the displacement (x) squared.

Thus work done = $1/2\, kx^2$ = change in elastic potential energy.

If a stretched or compressed spring is released, the stored potential energy is converted into kinetic energy.

For an oscillating spring: Total energy = $1/2\, kx^2 + 1/2\, mv^2$ = constant.

P12. Moments, mechanical advantage, levers and pulleys

a)   The moment (torque) of a force about a pivot is given by:
     Moment of force = force × perpendicular distance from pivot.
     For a lever balanced on a fulcrum (in equilibrium), the moments each side of the
     fulcrum are the same: $f_1d_1 = f_2d_2$.

b)   Mechanical advantage (MA) = load ÷ effort;
     (load = mechanical advantage × effort).
     Velocity ratio = distance effort moves ÷ distance load moves;
     (distance effort moves = velocity ratio × distance load moves).

c)   A lever is a practical application of moments. If $d_1 = 10\ d_2$, then a force of 1 N (f_1)
     will balance a load of 10 N (f_2).
     Mechanical advantage (MA) = load ÷ effort = × 10 in above.
     Velocity ratio = length of effort arm ÷ length resistance arm (× 10 above). Mechanical
     advantage = velocity ratio (no units).

d)   Classes of lever: these depend upon the relative positions of the pivot (fulcrum) the
     effort and the load.
     1st class: fulcrum between load and effort (eg seesaw; triceps):
     MA ≥ 1 (1st class can give the greatest magnification of force).
     2nd class: load between fulcrum and effort (eg wheelbarrow):
     MA > 1 (MA increases as the load approaches the fulcrum).
     3rd class: effort between fulcrum and load (eg biceps):
     MA < 1 (reduction in force = mechanical disadvantage; velocity ratio < 1 = magni-
     fication of movement).

e)   Mechanical (machine) efficiency: the units for moment of force are N m, as per
     work done, and since $f_1d_1 = f_2d_2$ no energy is lost if 100 per cent efficient (ie no
     friction/heat losses), so: Efficiency = work output ÷ work input × 100 per cent.
     This efficiency = mechanical advantage ÷ velocity ratio × 100 per cent.

f)   Pulley: Mechanical advantage = number of moving lines supporting the load.

P13. Pressure, buoyancy and flow

a)   Solids: Pressure = force ÷ area (N m^{-2} or pascals Pa); the units are identical to those
     for stress; that is, pressure = $mg ÷ A$.

b)   Liquids and gases: Pressure = force ÷ area = $mg ÷ A$ where the mass m = density of
     fluid (ρ) × volume (area × depth h);
     so Pressure = $pgAh ÷ A = pgh$; ie pressure is proportional to the depth below the
     surface and the density of the fluid.

c)   SI and non SI units for 1 atmosphere of pressure:
     i) SI: 1 atmosphere (atm) = 1 × 10^5 Pa = 100 kPa = 100 kN m^{-2};
     ii) non SI: 1 atm = 14.7 pounds per square inch (psi) = 760 mm mercury (Hg); = 760
     torr = 1 bar = 1000 millibars.

d) **Archimedes' principle:** a fully or partially immersed object experiences an upthrust equal to the weight of fluid displaced (and if submerged: volume object = volume displaced fluid (V_f)).

Upthrust (buoyancy) $= m_f g = \rho_f V_f g$ where $\rho_f =$ density of fluid.

Net force on an immersed object: $m_o g - \rho_f V_f g$; to float $= 0$, so:

floating bodies displace their own weight of fluid.

For water $\rho = 1$ g cm^{-3} ie weight in grams = volume in ml.

For example, a submerged object of volume 100 ml has an upthrust of 100 grams; a 100-gram mass that floats displaces 100 ml of water; a 100-gram mass that displaces 90 ml water sinks (net wt = 10 g).

e) Fluid flow and the continuity equation: fluids can be considered to be incompressible so the volume of fluid exiting a pipe must equal the volume of fluid entering it, per unit time.

Flow rate = vol per sec (cm^3 s^{-1}) = area (cm^2) × velocity (cm s^{-1}).

Thus $A_1 V_1 = A_2 V_2$; inverse law: velocity up at narrow sections.

f) Bernoulli's equation for fluid flow (conservation of energy):

P (pipe pressure energy) $+ \rho g h$ (PE; static head) $+ 1/2 \rho v^2$ (KE) = **constant** (velocity up at narrow cross sections = pressure down).

P14. Gas laws

a) Boyle's law: p proportional to $1/V$ ie pV = constant; $p_1 V_1 = p_2 V_2$.

Charles' law: V proportional to T ie V/T = constant; $V_1/T_1 = V_2/T_2$.

Gas law: p proportional to T ie p/T = constant; $p_1/T_1 = p_2/T_2$.

(T absolute: kelvin = °Celsius + 273; at T = 0 °K the pressure and volume of a gas are theoretically zero.)

b) Ideal gas equation (universal gas law): pV/T = constant;

or $p_1 V_1/T_1 = p_2 V_2/T_2$.

For example, a mass of gas occupying 1 L at 127 °C is cooled to 27 °C and the pressure on the gas is halved. What is the new volume?

$p_1 V_1/T_1 = p_2 V_2/T_2$; we have $V_1 = 1$, $T_1 = 400$ K, $T_2 = 300$ K; inserting these values gives $p_1 \times 1/400 = 0.5 p_1 \times V_2/300$ (T kelvin).

Finally: $0.5 V_2 = 300 \div 400 = 0.75$, giving new volume $V_2 = 1.5$ L.

c) Avagadro's law: PV = nRT (R is the universal gas constant; n = no of moles = weight in grams ÷ molecular weight).

One mole of any gas occupies 22.4 litres at STP (where standard temperature and pressure is 0 °C and 1 atm). Note that one mole of any gas occupies 24 litres at RTP (room temperature and pressure).

d) Dalton's law of partial pressures: $P_{total} = p_1 + p_2 + p_3$ etc.

For example, for air (nitrogen, oxygen, carbon dioxide): $P_{air} = pN_2 + pO_2 + pCO_2 + ...$

Composition of air: $N_2 = 78$ per cent; $O_2 = 21$ per cent; $CO_2 = 0.03$ per cent.

$P_{air} = 100$ kPa; so $pN_2 = 78$ kPa; $pO_2 = 21$ kPa; $pCO_2 = 0.03$ kPa.

e)   Gas transport (eg the lungs): at a constant temperature:
      Henry's law: the solubility of a gas in contact with a liquid is proportional to its partial pressure.
      Graham's law: the rate of diffusion of a gas is inversely proportional to the square root of its molecular mass.
      Fick's first law: the rate of diffusion of a gas (across a membrane) is proportional to the surface area and the concentration gradient (difference in partial pressures across membrane), and inversely proportional to the distance (membrane thickness).

P15. Heat and energy

a)   Specific heat capacity (c) of a substance is the number of joules of heat energy (Q) required to raise the temperature of 1 g of the substance by 1 K. For water, $c = 4.2 \, J \, g^{-1} \, K^{-1}$.
      The energy needed to raise m grams of a substance by ΔT degrees (K or °C) is given by: heat energy $Q = mc\Delta T$ joules.
      For example, the heat energy required raise the temperature of 1 L of water from 25 °C to boiling point is given by: $Q = mc\Delta T = 1000 \times 4.2 \times (100 - 25) \, J = 315 \, kJ$.

b)   Latent heat of vaporization (L) of a substance is the number of joules of heat energy (Q) required to change 1 g of the substance from liquid to vapour without change in temperature. For water, $L = 2260 \, J \, g^{-1}$.
      The energy needed to convert m grams of a liquid to m grams of vapour at the same temperature is given by: heat of vaporization $= mL$ joules.
      For example, the heat energy required to convert 1 L of water at 100 °C to steam at 100 °C is given by: $Q = mL = 1000 \times 2260 \, J = 2260 \, kJ$ (ie seven times more energy than is required to reach boiling point).

c)   Latent heat of fusion (L) of a substance is the number of joules of heat energy (Q) required to change 1 g of the substance from solid to liquid without change in temperature. For water, $L = 334 \, J \, g^{-1}$. The energy need to converted m grams of a solid to m grams of a liquid at the same temperature is given by: heat of fusion $= mL$ joules.

d)   Heat transfer: conduction (solids), convection (liquids; currents) and radiation (electromagnetic waves; black bodies emit and absorb the most wavelengths).

P16. Waves (light and sound)

a)   Two types: *transverse* (light and all electromagnetic waves; peaks, troughs) and *longitudinal* (eg sound; spring motion). Waves can be reflected at barriers (eg light at mirrors) and diffracted (bent) at corners and slits (eg sound waves).

b) $v = f\lambda$; v is the wave's speed (m s^{-1}), f its frequency (Hz; cycles s^{-1}), λ its wavelength (m). For light, $c = 3 \times 10^8 \, m \, s^{-1} = f\lambda$.

One wavelength is the distance between corresponding points on two successive waves (eg adjacent peaks), which is one cycle. Time for one cycle is the period (T) so we have $f = 1/T$ and $v = \lambda/T$. Amplitude (a) of wave = *half the height between peak and trough*. Doppler: moving source; $v_s = 340$ m s^{-1} for sound (constant); waves appears shorter, frequency higher. Wave energy: $E = fh$ where E is in joules, f in hertz; h is Planck's constant (6.63×10^{-34} J Hz^{-1} or J s).

c) Reflection: angle of incidence (i) = angle of reflection (r); no change in velocity (same medium).

d) Refraction: angle of incidence (i) ≠ angle of refraction (r); change in velocity (medium 1 to medium 2), wave bends (except when the wave strikes perpendicular to the boundary; then $i = r = 0°$). Refractive index (n): $n = \sin i/\sin r$ and $v_2/v_1 = \lambda_2/\lambda_1 = n_1/n_2 = \sin i/\sin r$; thus $n_1\sin r = n_2 \sin i$.
Refractive index (n) for light in a medium is given by $n = c/v$ where c is the speed of light in a vacuum and v is the speed of light in the medium. A prism splits light because the constituent wavelengths travel at different speeds in glass but not in air. For example, air$_1$ to glass$_2$: light slows down, wavelength increases and light bends towards the normal.
Total internal reflection occurs when the critical angle of incidence is exceeded and all the light is reflected. The critical angle is given by: $i_{crit} = \sin^{-1}(n_1/n_2)$; (glass to air $n_2 > n_1$; $n_1 \sin r = n_2 \sin i$ with $r = 90°$, ie light travels parallel to interface).

e) Lens formula: $1/u + 1/v = 1/f$; Lens magnification $M = v/u$ = ratio of object distance (v) to image distance (u); f = focal length; $1/f = D$ (units = m^{-1} or dioptres) = lens power.

f) Eye: short-sighted: distant light focused short of retina (lens too thick, ie too powerful; muscles not relaxed enough). Long-sighted: near light focused behind retina (lens too thin, ie not powerful enough; muscles too weak).

P17. Electrostatics, capacitance and electricity

a) Coulomb's law: the electric forces of attraction (opposite charges) and repulsion (like charges) between two charged bodies (q_1 and q_2) are proportional to the inverse square of the distance of separation (r) and the product of the charges (distance × 2 then force × 1/4) $F = k\, q_1 q_2/r^2$ (k is the constant of proportionality). Positive charge flows outward; negative inward.

b) Potential difference (volt): 1 V = 1 joule per coulomb.

c) Capacitance (farad): capacitors are two parallel plates with equal and opposite charges ($\pm Q$), separated by insulating material (*dielectric that supports an electrostatic field*). Capacitance = charge stored per volt: $C = Q/V$ or $Q = CV$. More charge is stored as the voltage increases, the plate separation decreases, the plate area increases and the dielectric constant of the insulator between plates increases. Energy (E joules) stored between the plates: $E = \frac{1}{2} CV^2$ (or the area under a charge voltage graph). Capacitors discharge exponentially; that is to say, a very high current flows at first, dropping away to zero (half-life $t_{1/2}$: 1/2 at t, 1/2 × 1/2 at $2t$), and across a resistor R, $t_{1/2}$ (s) = $\log_e$ (2) × RC = 0.693 × RC (logarithmic charge/discharge).

d) Current (I), voltage (V) and power (W):
amps = coulombs per second (C s^{-1}).
Thus 1 amp × 1 second = 1 coulomb of charge;
power = voltage × current = J C^{-1} × C s^{-1} = J s^{-1} = watt;
$W = VI$, and watt (J s^{-1}) × time (s) = energy (J) so:
energy = power × time (kW hours for household electricity).

e) Ohm's law (resistance), and power losses:
$V = IR$ (voltage current for a constant resistance R measured in ohms). Power loss (as heat energy) in a conductor of resistance R: $W = I^2R$ (substitute $V = IR$ in $W = VI$) so increase V to reduce I^2R losses (National Grid = 400 kV). Furthermore, R proportional to length of wire and inversely proportional to cross-sectional area (diam^2); thus longer, thinner wires offer more resistance.

P18. Kirchhoff's circuit laws, resistors and capacitors

a) Kirchhoff current law: the current entering any point (node) in a circuit equals the current leaving it: $I_1 + I_2 + I_3 = I_4 + I_5 + I_6$.

b) Kirchhoff's voltage law (loop law): the sum of the changes in potential around any closed loop is zero; that is, the potential differences across any resistors must equal the potential difference across the battery (the latter is the electromotive force (EMF) of the battery ('battery voltage')). $V_{bat} = V_1 + V_2 + V_3$.
Thus $V_{bat} - V_1 - V_2 - V_3 = 0$. For example, work clockwise around a loop with the electricity flowing from positive to negative.

c) Resistors series (joined end to end, one end only): $R_{tot} = R_1 + R_2 + R_3$.
For a closed loop: the resistors have the same current passing through each of them: $V_{bat} = IR_1 + IR_2 + IR_3 = V_1 + V_2 + V_3$.

d) Resistors in parallel (joined to each other at both ends); reciprocal law:
$1/R_{tot} = 1/R_1 + 1/R_2 + 1/R_3$.
In a closed loop: each resistor has the same potential difference (ie equal to the battery voltage V_{bat}) and the current divides accordingly:
$I = I_1 + I_2 + I_3$ so $V_{bat}/R_{tot} = V_{bat}/R_1 + V_{bat}/R_2 + V_{bat}/R_3$.
NB: R_{tot} is always less than the smallest individual resistance.

e) Capacitors joined: the rules for combining capacitors are the opposite of those for combining resistors (use the reciprocal law for capacitors joined in series and the sum law for capacitors joined in parallel).

f) Battery cells: for two (or more) cells wired in series (positive to negative), add the voltages together to find the resultant voltage. For two cells (of the same voltage) wired in parallel (positive to positive / negative to negative), the voltage remains unchanged. However, twice the amount of current can be supplied.

P19. Electromagnetism and electromagnetic induction

a) Right-hand rule: a conductor (wire) carrying an electric current creates a magnetic field (flux) that radiates out in concentric circles. Grasp the wire with your right hand and point the thumb in the direction of the current; the magnetic field lines follow the rotation of your fingers around the wire.

b) Magnetic force on a wire in a magnetic field is perpendicular to both the direction of current and the magnetic field; (open the fingers in a) above; palm of the hand faces the direction of force). Field strength (tesla T) is proportional to the current and inversely proportional to the distance from the wire. One T produces a force of 1 N per ampere per metre of wire.

Example i) motor: one side of the loops is attracted to the north poles of the magnets and the other sides to the south poles (rotates).

Example ii) solenoid: magnetic field runs parallel to the axis, giving north and south poles similar to a bar magnet.

c) Electromagnetic induction (opposite of b)) in a conductor is an emf (and current) induced in a wire loop when the magnetic field changes (eg pushing a bar magnet into (or out of) a wire loop (or rotating the magnet), or changing the field strength in an electromagnet near the loop); current flows in a direction that opposes the change producing it. Examples include AC electrical generators.

d) Transformers (electromagnetic induction): the primary AC voltage (V_1) is stepped down (or up) to the secondary AC voltage (V_2) by a factor equal to the ratio of the number of turns: secondary coil (N_2) to primary coil (N_1):

$V_2/V_1 = N_2/N_1$ or $V_2 N_1 = V_1 N_2$.

Step-down transformer if N_2/N_1 less than 1. Step-up transformer if N_2/N_1 is greater than 1. The secondary power out equals the primary power in: $V_1 I_1 = V_2 I_2$; thus if the voltage is stepped down, the current is stepped up and vice versa; if the turns are stepped down, the current is stepped up and vice versa: $I_1 N_1 = I_2 N_2$.

P20. Radioactive decay

a) Alpha, beta and gamma rays. *Alpha* particles are positively charged helium ions (helium atoms minus two electrons = nucleus = two protons and two neutrons); low penetration, stopped by paper; highly ionizing. *Beta* particles are high-energy electrons, stopped by thin aluminium; moderately ionizing. *Gamma* rays are high-energy photons (electromagnetic radiation; E = f h); high penetration, stopped by several centimetres of dense metal (eg lead); weakly ionizing.

For example, alpha decay: (lose charge +2, mass 4): $^{238}_{92}U$ to $^{234}_{90}Th + ^{4}_{2}He$;

beta decay: (lose charge −1, mass 0): $^{90}_{38}Sr$ to $^{90}_{39}Y + ^{0}_{-1}e$;

(mass change = 0; neutron decays to a proton, emits an electron);

gamma decay (charge and mass unchanged): $^{12}_{6}C$ to $^{12}_{7}N + \gamma$ ray.

b) Half-life $(T_{1/2})$: radioactive isotopes (radioisotopes) decay spontaneously to produce alpha or beta particles. The number of disintegrations is proportional to the number of active atoms left (exponential decay). For example, radioactive iodine (iodine-131) can be used to treat thyroid cancer. The half-life is eight days. The number of active atoms continues to halve for every half-life elapsed from the time of preparation (from time/day 0).

For example, what percentage of a sample of radioactive iodine-131 (half-life = 8 days) remains undecayed (ie active) after eight weeks?

8 weeks = 56 days; 56 days ÷ 8 days per half-life = 7 half-lives; the fraction remaining is: $1/2 \times 1/2 \times 1/2 \times 1/2 \times 1/2 \times 1/2 \times 1/2$ (or $(1/2)^7$) = 1/128 = 0.78 per cent (to 2 sf).

c) One becquerel (Bq) = 1 atom disintegrating per second (1 count per second).

d) One electron volt (eV) is the kinetic energy acquired by an electron losing one volt of potential.

Physics review questions

Q1. (P4c) A man falls from a ladder and lands on the ground exactly 0.5 seconds later. How far did he fall? Gravity is 10 m s^{-2}.

(hint: $ut + \frac{1}{2} at^2$)

Answer ☐

Q2. (P6e) A stone is thrown horizontally from a vertical cliff at a speed of 20 metres per second. The cliff is 30 metres above sea level and the stone hits the sea after 2.5 seconds. How far from the base of the cliff is the stone when it hits the sea? $g =$ 10 m s^{-2}?

(hint: treat horizontal and vertical motion separately)

Answer ☐

Q3.   (P7a,b,e,f) A rightward force is applied to a 10-kg object to move it across a rough surface at constant velocity. The coefficient of friction between the object and the surface is 0.2.

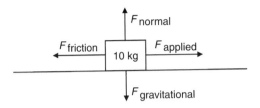

Use the diagram to determine to the following forces: ($g = 10$ m s^{-2})

A.   gravitational force = ...
B.   normal force = ...
C.   friction force = ...
D.   applied force = ...

(hint: Newton's three laws: acceleration?)

Answer [   ]

Q4.   (P7c,g) A parachutist of mass 80 kg reaches a terminal velocity of 50 m s^{-1}, at which point he throws a ball vertically downwards at a velocity of 20 m s^{-1} relative to him. What is the acceleration of the ball vertically downwards relative to the parachutist immediately after it has been thrown? (1 kg = 10 N.)

A.   0 m s^{-2}
B.   70 m s^{-1}
C.   30 m s^{-1}
D.   10 m s^{-2}

(hint: units)

Answer [   ]

Q5.   (P8b) A hydraulic ramp can lift a vehicle weighing 6 tonnes to a height of 2 metres in 50 seconds. What is the power of the ramp in kilowatts? (1 kg = 10 N.)

(hint: rate of work)

Answer [   ]

Q6.   (P8c) At a hydroelectric pumped storage scheme, the reservoir is 500 metres above the turbine house. What is the velocity of the water when it arrives at the turbines? Neglect energy losses on the descent and take g to be 10 m s^{-2}.

(hint: conservation of energy)

Answer [   ]

Q7.   (P8a, 17c) An electric scooter has a mass of 100 kg (including its user). The force required to overcome its rolling resistance is 10 per cent of its weight. It is driven by a 24-volt electric motor that takes its power from batteries that hold 2×10^5 coulombs of charge. What is the range of the scooter in kilometres? (1 kg = 10 N.)

(hint: work done by scooter = work done by batteries)

Answer [   ]

Q8.   (P16b) The frequency of middle C on the piano is 260 Hz. If sound waves travel at a speed of 338 m s^{-1}, what is the wavelength of middle C in centimetres?

A.   125 cm
B.   130 cm
C.   132 cm
D.   131 cm
E.   128 cm

(hint: units; cycles per sec)

Answer [   ]

Q9.   (P7e, 10a,b) A 12-gauge shotgun weighing 6 kg fires 30 g of lead shot at 400 m s^{-1}. What is the speed of recoil of the gun?

(hint: momentum)

Answer [   ]

Q10.   (P17d) What is the power of an electric kettle if the heating element has a resistance of 23 ohm? Take mains voltage to be 230 volts.

A.   2.2 kW
B.   2.3 kW
C.   2.5 kW
D.   3 kW
E.   1.5 kW

(hint: Ohm's law)

Answer [   ]

Q11. (P17d) How much energy does a 3-kilowatt electric kettle consume when it is connected to a 240-volt supply for three minutes?

(hint: ignore voltage)

Answer ☐

Q12. (P5) Which pair of the graphs below could show the motion of the same object?

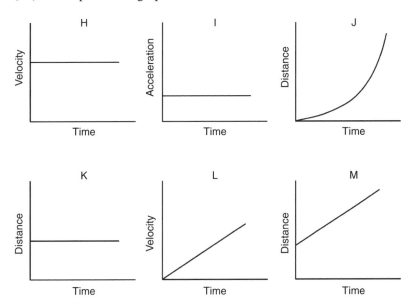

A. L and M
B. H and K
C. L and M
D. J and L
E. J and M

Answer ☐

4

Chemistry review

C1. Atoms, electron configuration and valency

a) Atomic number: the number of protons in the atom

Neutral atoms: number of protons (+) = number of electrons (–).

b) Atomic mass

Number of protons + number of neutrons; usually more than twice atomic number (C, N, O, S, Si, Mg, Ca are exactly ×2).

The atomic mass is written above the atomic number, eg $^{12}_{6}C$.

c) Electron config: quantum number (n) of electron shells

$n = 1$ (2 electrons max in 1 subshell type) $1s^2$.
$n = 2$ (8 electrons max in 2 subshell types) $2s^2\,2p^6$.

$n = 3$: (18 electrons max in 3 subshell types) $3s^2 3p^6 3d^{10}$.
$n = 4$: (32 electrons max in 4 subshell types) $4s^2 4p^6 4d^{10} 4f^{14}$.

s-p-d-f; fill the lowest energy levels first s2, p6, d10, f14:
for example, iron: atomic number 26: $1s^2 2s^2 2p^6 3s^2 3p^6 4s^2 3d^6$;
silver: atomic number 47: $1s^2 2s^2 2p^6 3s^2 3p^6 4s^2 3d^{10} 4p^6 5s^2 4d^9$.

d) *Valency*

The number of valence (outer) shell electrons an atom must lose or gain to achieve a valence octet (8 = noble gas structure). Atoms combine to achieve full shells.

For example, sodium: atomic number 11: 2 + 8 +1 ($1s^2 2s^2 2p^6 3s^1$);
chlorine: atomic number 17: 2 + 8 + 7 ($1s^2 2s^2 2p^6 3s^2 3p^5$).

$Na^+ = 2 + 8$; $Cl^- = 2 + 8 + 8$. For Na: $1s^2 2s^2 2p^6 3s^1$ = ground state;
$1s^2 2s^2 2p^6$ = ionized state; $1s^2 2s^1 2p^6 3s^2$ = (photon) excited state.

e) *Periodic table*

Groups = vertical columns; periods = rows; periods correspond with principal quantum number; same group elements have the same valency/similar properties. Reactivity:

Group 1: alkali metals: Li < Na < K < Rb < Cs; (form cations^{+1}).
Group 2: alkaline earth metals: Be < Mg < Ca < Sr < Ba (form cations^{+2}).
Group 13: B, Al (form cations^{+3}).
Group 14: C, Si.
Group 15: N, P (form anions^{-3}).
Group 16: O, S (form anions^{-2}).
Group 17: halogens: F > Cl > Br > I; (form anions^{-1}).
Group 18: (or 0) noble gases: He, Ne, Ar (inert, octet; eg 2,8,8).

Charges balance in compounds, eg calcium chloride $Ca^{2+}(Cl^-)_2$.

C2. Periodic table

C2 Periodic Table (short form; 4 periods: 1 to 4 electron shells; 18 groups)

smaller atoms, more electronegative (left to right and bottom to top) ⟶

	1	2		d-block									13	14	15	16	17	18
1	$^{1}_{1}H$																	$^{4}_{2}He$
2	$^{7}_{3}Li$	$^{9}_{4}Be$											$^{11}_{5}B$	$^{12}_{6}C$	$^{14}_{7}N$	$^{16}_{8}O$	$^{19}_{9}F$	$^{20}_{10}Ne$
3	$^{23}_{11}Na$	$^{24}_{12}Mg$											$^{27}_{13}Al$	$^{28}_{14}Si$	$^{31}_{15}P$	$^{32}_{16}S$	$^{35.5}_{17}Cl$	$^{40}_{18}Ar$
4	$^{39}_{19}K$	$^{40}_{20}Ca$	$^{45}_{21}Sc$	$^{48}_{22}Ti$	$^{51}_{23}V$	$^{52}_{24}Cr$	$^{55}_{25}Mn$	$^{56}_{26}Fe$	$^{59}_{27}Co$	$^{59}_{28}Ni$	$^{64}_{29}Cu$	$^{65}_{30}Zn$	$^{70}_{31}Ga$	$^{73}_{32}Ge$	$^{75}_{33}As$	$^{79}_{34}Se$	$^{80}_{35}Br$	$^{84}_{36}Kr$

p-block · s-block · non-metals

s-block (alkali metals; soft metals, very reactive, not found in the free state, reducing agents (donate electrons), dissolve in water to give alkaline solutions; alkaline earth metals; light metals, water insoluble)

p-block (eg halogens; metal halides are crystalline, water soluble, oxidizing agents eg F (accept electrons) (eg noble gases; colourless and unreactive with stable electronic configurations (octet))

d-block (transition metals; high strength, high melting points, form coloured compounds)

Chlorine-35.5 is the weighted average of two **isotopes** Cl-35 (18 neutrons) and Cl-37 (20 neutrons)

Definitions: Cl is an **element** made up of **atoms**; Cl_2 is a **molecule** (a discrete unit of atoms bonded); an unreacted **mixture** of H_2 and Cl_2 exposed to sunlight react to from a **compound** (HCl); Cl^{-1} is an **ion**

C3. Bonding: electrovalent (ionic), covalent and metallic

a) Electrovalent (ionic)

Atoms exchange electrons to give ions that form strong electrostatic bonds (positive cations, negative anions). Bond strength increases with increasing charge and smaller ions (fluoride smallest anion, lithium smallest cation). Properties: inorganic salts with giant lattice structures (ionic crystals); solid at room temperature with high melting and boiling points (strong bonds); conduct electricity when molten or dissolved in water (ionic solution); iodides most soluble (dissociate) in water, fluorides least soluble. Insoluble in organic solvents. Examples: groups 1, 2 metal halides (Na^+Cl^-, $Ca^{2+}F_2^-$).

b) Covalent

Atoms share one or more electron pairs to achieve full shells (eight outer electrons) as per the following diatomic and triatomic *molecules*: H_2, Cl_2, F_2, N_2, O_2, CO; H_2O, H_2S, CO_2, NO_2.

The number of shared electron pairs is the molecular covalency.

Carbon has four outer electrons ($2s^2\ 2p^2$) and attains a valency of four ($2s^2\ 2p^6$) by sharing with another four pairs; for example CH_4 = four single covalent bonds, CO_2 = two double covalent bonds. Properties: opposite of ionic; low melting/boiling points (eg gas); non-conducting; 'like dissolves like' so some are soluble in organic (C-based) solvents such as ethanol, but insoluble in water.

c) *Metallic*

Atoms are packed together tightly (like snooker balls in a triangle), surrounded by a sea of electrons (de-localized).

Properties: most have high melting points (strong bonds); good electrical and thermal conductivity (highly mobile outer electrons); high strength, especially when alloyed with other metals (eg brass = 60 per cent copper and 40 per cent tin).

d) *Electronegativity*

This is the ability of atoms to attract electrons; concept links ionic and covalent bonding. A large difference (>2) favours ionic bonds (eg Cl high, Na low) whereas similar electronegativities favour covalent bonds (eg C, H); intermediate (eg Cl and H) form polar compounds that display both types of bonding (HCl is a covalent gas that forms aqueous ions).

C4. The mole and balancing chemical equations (reactions)

a) *Mole*

By *definition* one mole of any substance contains 6.022×10^{23} particles of the substance (Avogadro's number); for example, 'one mole of peanuts contains 6.022×10^{23} peanuts'. More usefully, 6.022×10^{23} atoms, ions or molecules is one mole of each. For an element, an amount in grams equal to the atomic mass contains one mole of atoms. For a molecule such as H_2O, one mole of H_2O contains two moles of H and one mole of O. The molecular mass of H_2O is $2 + 16 = 18$ so 18 grams of $H_2O = 1$ mole H_2O ($2 \times 6.022 \times 10^{23}$ atoms of H and $1 \times 6.022 \times 10^{23}$ atoms of O).

More generally: mass ÷ molecular mass = number of moles;

for example, 54 grams of water is $54 \div 18 = 3$ moles of water.

b) *Balancing chemical equations*

Atoms are neither created nor destroyed, so where we have same number of atoms on each side of the equation.

For example, $H_2 + O_2 = H_2O$ (unbalanced; two hydrogens + two oxygens on the left but two hydrogens + one oxygen on the right). We have one too many oxygen atoms on the left so to balance:

$H_2 + \frac{1}{2} O_2 = H_2O$ and normally written as $2H_2 + O_2 \rightarrow 2H_2O$.

For more complicated equations:

i)   Balance the atoms in the more complex molecules first. Try the molecule on the far left of the equation (balance the atoms in this molecule with the same atoms on the right of the equation).

ii) Balance the simpler molecules second, leaving the diatomic molecules (1 atom type) until the last (eg hydrogen, oxygen).

For example, in the combustion of propane with oxygen the following reaction takes place:

$C_3H_8 + O_2 \rightarrow CO_2 + H_2O$ (skeleton equation).

i) Starting with propane on the left; it has 3 carbon atoms to be balanced:
$C_3H_8 + O_2 \rightarrow 3CO_2 + H_2O$; now balance the 8 H atoms:
$C_3H_8 + O_2 \rightarrow 3CO_2 + 4H_2O$.

ii) Finally, balance the O atoms: $C_3H_8 + 5O_2 \rightarrow 3CO_2 + 4H_2O$
(3 carbon, 8 hydrogen and 10 oxygen atoms on each side).

C5. Types of chemical reaction

a) *neutralization*

- acid (H^+) + base (OH^-) → metal salt + water.

  (base = metal oxide/hydroxide and if soluble → alkali eg NaOH.)

- acid + carbonate/hydrogen carbonate → metal salt + water + CO_2.

- acid + ammonia → ammonium salt + water.

- acid + metal → metal salt + hydrogen.

b) *oxidation-reduction (redox)*

For every oxidation there is a corresponding reduction.

- Oxidation = add oxygen/remove hydrogen/loss of electrons.
- Reduction = remove oxygen/add hydrogen/gain of electrons.

('OILRIG' – oxidation is loss; reduction is gain).

For a redox reaction: valency = oxidation number (+ or –) and the charges balance on either side of the equation.

- $Fe + CuSO_4 \rightarrow FeSO_4 + Cu$; split into half-reactions:
- $Fe \rightarrow Fe^{2+} + 2e^-$ (oxidation; Fe oxidation number 0 to +2);
- $Cu^{2+} + 2e^- \rightarrow Cu$ (reduction; Cu oxidation number +2 to 0);
- Fe (reducing agent) oxidized; Cu^{2+} (oxidizing agent) reduced.

c) *Displacement reaction*

Single: $Fe + CuSO_4 \rightarrow FeSO_4 + Cu$ (replacement; also a redox);
Double: $FeS + 2HCl \rightarrow FeCl_2 + H_2S$ (2 new compounds formed).

d) *Combustion reaction*

The oxidation of each element in the compound; for example, a hydrocarbon fuel burning in O_2.

e) *Composition, decomposition and dissociation*

Composition (synthesis) $A + B \rightarrow AB$; decomposition: $AB \rightarrow A + B$; dissociation: $AB \rightarrow A^+ + B^-$ (eg NaCl in water).

Composition one way, decomposition the other: $2H + O_2 = H_2O$.

f) *Substitution*

Swap an atom, ion or group in a molecule; for example, swap a hydrogen linked to a carbon: $CH_4 + Cl_2 \rightarrow CH_3Cl + HCl$.

g) *Hydrolysis/condensation*

Hydrolysis = add water molecule; condensation = remove water molecule.

C6. Concentration and pH; reaction rates

a) *Concentration: moles per dm³ (litre)*

1 mole of solute in 1 litre of solution = 1.0 molar (M) solution. Normality (N) is used with acids (or alkalis) to reflect the number of protons (or hydroxide ions) per litre.
For example $1.0\,M\,H_2SO_4 = 2.0\,N\,H_2SO_4$; $1.0\,M = 1.0\,N$ for HCl, NaOH.

Medicine uses millimoles per litre (mmol/L); for example blood: glucose 4 to 6 mmol/L, Na 135–145 mmol/L, K 3.5–5 mmol/L, cholesterol 5 mmol/L. (NB 'Normal saline' for infusions is 0.9 per cent weight/volume (w/v) NaCl (ie 0.9 g NaCl per 100 ml of water; not Normality)).

b) *pH scale ('potential of hydrogen')*

$pH = -\log_{10}$ moles H^+/L.
pH ranges from pH 0 (strong acid) to pH 14 (strong alkali).

- pH $H_2O = 7$ (neutral). Log scale ($\times 10$, $\times 100$, $\times 1000\ H^+$ etc).
- $0.1\,M$ HCl, $pH = -\log_{10} 0.1 = 1$; $0.01\,M$ HCl, $pH = -\log_{10} 0.01 = 2\,0$.
- $001\,M$ HCl, $pH = -\log_{10} 0.001 = 3.0$; pH gastric HCl approx 1 to 2.
- $H_2O = H^+ + OH^-$; $[H^+] = 10^{-7}$ $pH = -\log_{10} 10^{-7} = 7$ (neutral).

$[H^+] = [OH^-] = 10^{-7}$; equilibrium constant K_w = product of the concentrations, that is to say $K_w = [H^+][OH^-] = 10^{-14}$ so if add acid (H^+) to water pH goes down and pOH (hydroxide ions) goes up; eg if pH = 5, pOH = 9.

c) *Reaction rates*

For $A + B$ = product; rate = $k\,[A]^x\,[B]^y$.

i) Rate: product of concentrations A, B and the *order* of the reaction:

zero-order reaction ($x + y = 0$): rate = k (k is the rate constant);

first-order reaction ($x + y = 1$): rate = $k[A]$ or $k\,[B]$;

second-order reaction ($x + y = 2$): rate = $k[A]^2$, $k\,[B]^2$ or $k[A][B]$.

ii) Rate increases with increasing temperature (approx × 2 for every 10 °C rise in temperature). Molecules have more kinetic energy; a greater proportion overcome the activation energy (ie the height of the peak on a potential-energy/reaction graph).

iii) Rate increases in the presence of a catalyst (eg enzyme) that lowers the activation energy for the reaction. Faster equilibrium but position unchanged. Catalysts not consumed.

iv) Rate increases with greater surface area (eg powder).

C7. Exothermic and endothermic reactions; Le Chatelier's principle

a) *exothermic reactions*

Heat energy is released. Enthalpy of reaction is negative; $\Delta H < 0$ (gives off heat/lost to surroundings) Examples: combustion and bond making (gets hotter):

$$CH_{4(g)} + 2O_{2(g)} \rightarrow CO_{2(g)} + 2H_2O_{(g)} \quad \Delta H = -890 \text{ kJ mol}^{-1};$$
$$N_{2(g)} + 3H_{2(g)} \rightarrow 2NH_{3(g)} \quad \Delta H = -90 \text{ kJ mol}^{-1}.$$

b) *endothermic reactions*

Heat energy is absorbed. Enthalpy of reaction is positive; $\Delta H > 0$ (heat added from surroundings). Examples: liquid to gas and bond breaking (cools down):

$$H_2O_{(l)} \rightarrow H_2O_{(g)} \quad \Delta H = +43 \text{ kJ mol}^{-1}.$$
$$2NH_{3(g)} \rightarrow N_{2(g)} + 3H_{2(g)} \quad \Delta H = +90 \text{ kJ mol}^{-1}.$$

Reversible reaction: $N_{2(g)} + 3H_{2(g)} = 2NH_{3(g)}$ (a dynamic equilibrium):
that is, exothermic to the right and endothermic to the left.

c) *Le Chatelier's principle*

For a system in equilibrium, when a change is made to the conditions the equilibrium will shift so as to oppose the change.

■ Temperature: raise it and the reaction shifts to absorb heat; lower it and the reaction shifts to produce more heat.

Endothermic reaction: raise the temperature, equilibrium moves to the left to absorb excess heat (more $N_{2(g)} + 3H_{2(g)}$).
Exothermic reactions: lower the temperature and the equilibrium moves to the right to produce more heat (more NH_3).

■ Pressure: increase it and the reaction shifts to lower it (by reducing the number of molecules/volume) and vice versa.
For example $N_{2(g)} + 3H_{2(g)} = 2NH_{3(g)}$ (1 mole + 3 moles = 2 moles).
Increase the pressure to produce more NH_3.

■ Concentration: increase the concentration of a molecule and the reaction shifts to decrease it and vice versa. Add N_2, H_2 or remove NH_3 and the equilibrium shifts to the right (more NH_3). NB: do not confuse equilibrium ('how far') and reaction rates ('how fast'); in NH_3 production, a low temperature would favour a greater proportion (yield) but the reaction is too slow; so 500 °C, 300 atmospheres, add a catalyst to increase the rate (no effect on equilibrium) and remove the NH_3 as it is produced).

C8. Solids, liquids, gases; changes of state; themochemistry

a) Gases, liquids, solids

i) **Gases:** very low density; no shape, weak bonds; particles diffuse to fill any volume; easy to compress. Pressure of a gas is a linear function of temperature. *PV* is constant at constant temperature (see Physics P14).

ii) **Liquids:** much more dense than gases and usually less dense than when in the solid state (water/ice is the notable exception). Constant volume (incompressible for most practical purposes, eg hydraulic rams); take on the shape of the container; particles are bonded locally. Expand much less than gases when heated.

iii) **Solids:** usually the most dense state and incompressible, though depends on the structure. Strong bonds between particles, so take on a rigid form. Expand less than liquids on heating. All metals, mercury excepted, are solids at room temperature

b) Changes of state (gas, liquid and solid)

i) **Solid to liquid, liquid to solid:** solid to liquid = melting point (heat energy absorbed) and liquid to solid = freezing point (reverse of melting at the same temperature, heat released); liquid to gas = vaporization (heat absorbed) and gas to liquid = condensation (heat released); also solid to gas = sublimation; gas to solid = deposition.
Examples: ice at 0 °C melts to water at 0 °C with heat in, and water at 0 °C freezes to (wet) ice at 0 °C with heat out; water boils at 100 °C and vaporizes to steam at 100 °C with heat in, and steam at 100 °C condenses to water at 100 °C with heat out; dry ice (solid carbon dioxide) sublimes to carbon dioxide gas. NB: evaporation is vaporization at the surface of the liquid, whereas boiling is vaporization from within the body of the liquid as well.

ii) **Temperature versus pressure graph:** solid to liquid to gas with increasing temperature and gas to liquid to solid with increasing pressure (which increases the boiling point). Triple point: all three states in equilibrium; critical temperature: above this a gas cannot be condensed to liquid by increased pressure.

iii) **Impurities:** impurities such as grit or salt lower the freezing point (snow melts in the presence of rock salt) and increase the boiling point.

C9. Electrochemistry, reactivity series and electrolysis

a) *Electrochemistry*

Chemical reactions can give rise to electricity (batteries) and vice versa (electrolysis of electrolytes).

i)   Conductors: metals, and carbon in the form of graphite.

ii)   Insulators: non-metals (glass/ceramics, polymers, rubber).

iii) Semi-conductors: (between i, ii) silicon 'chips' (metalloids).

iv) Electrolytes: conduct electricity when molten or dissolved in water (eg salts, acids, alkalis).

v)   Electrodes: positive (anode) and negative (cathode) terminals.

b) *Electrolysis*

When an electrical current is passed through an electrolyte, cations migrate to the cathode, where electrons are added (reduction), and anions migrate to the anode, where electrons are removed/lost (oxidation); an example is the electrolytic extraction of Al: molten cryolite (sodium aluminium fluoride at 1000 °C, 5 volt, 30 kA):

■   at the cathode (negative): $Al^{3+} + 3e^- = Al$ (charges balance);

■   at the anode (positive): $2O^{2-} = O_2 + 4e^-$ (charges balance).

Faraday's law of electrolysis states that the amount of aluminium deposited at the cathode, or oxygen liberated at the anode, is directly proportional to the amount of current passed.

1 faraday (F) = 1 mole of electrons = 96 500 coulombs.
    So 3 moles of electrons (3 faradays) will deposit 1 mole of aluminium (27 g) from 1 mole of Al^{3+} cations and 0.75 moles of oxygen (12g) from 2 moles of O^{2-} anions.
1 coulomb of charge = 1 amp for 1 second so 96 500 ampere seconds will deposit one-third of a mole of aluminium (9 g).

c) *Reactivity series*

i) K, Na, Ca, Mg, Al, C, Zn, Fe, Sn, Pb, H, Cu, Ag, Au, Pt. More electropositive (reactive) metals displace less electropositive (more noble) metals from solution (eg iron displaces copper from copper sulphate).

ii) Electrolysis of salts in water: metals above/before H (more reactive) are not formed at the cathode; instead H_2 is discharged. At the anode O_2 is discharged, except for halides salts (when halogen is discharged instead). Summary: O_2 at anode unless halide salt (halogen discharged); H_2 at cathode, unless Cu^{2+} (then Cu deposited).

iii) Electrolysis of acids: dilute solutions give H_2 and O_2 (2:1 volume ratio); concentrated hydrochloric acid gives H_2 and Cl_2 (1:1 volume ratio).

C10. Carbon (organic) chemistry; fractional distillation

a) *Allotropes of carbon*

Carbon has three main allotropes: graphite, carbon and fullerenes (buckyball); in other words, the same element occurs in a different physical form with a different molecular structure.

i) Graphite: an electrically conducting soft powder; giant non-crystalline sheets that slide over each other (three strong covalent bonds in 2-d hexagonal planes and one weak bond between planes).

ii) Diamond: very hard; giant structure with four strong covalent bonds.

iii) Fullerenes: hollow spherical clusters of carbon atoms such as C_{60}.

b) *Alkanes, alkenes, alkynes*

i) Alkanes (C_nH_{2n+2}): carbon–carbon single bonds (eg methane CH_4, propane C_3H_8); saturated hydrocarbons (C, H only); combust completely in air to produce water and carbon dioxide, or carbon monoxide if combustion incomplete (lack of oxygen).

ii) Alkenes (C_nH_{2n}): carbon–carbon double bonds (eg ethane, C_2H_4).

iii) Alkynes (C_nH_{2n-2}): carbon–carbon triple bonds (eg propyne, C_3H_4).

c) *Fractional distillation*

Fractional distillation (ie evaporation and condensation) separates a mixture (compounds that are not combined chemically) into its constituents according to their boiling points.

In the fractional distillation of crude oil, the alkanes with shorter carbon chains (<10 carbons) are lighter, boil off first and are highly flammable (eg propane); the larger molecules (carbon chains > 20) are less volatile, highly viscous (flow less easily) and are more difficult to ignite (eg heavy fuel oil, bitumen).

i) Cracking (with steam) breaks less useful, longer hydrocarbon chains into more useful shorter chains; for example, heavy fuel oil to petrol.

ii) Polymerization of alkenes (unsaturated hydrocarbons) builds short chains to long chains; for example, ethene to polyethene (polyethylene).

iii) Reforming changes straight chain hydrocarbons into aromatic hydrocarbons; for example, hexane to benzene (same number of carbons).

iv) Isomers have the same formula but a different arrangement of atoms; for example, 2-methyl-propane is an isomer of butane; both are C_4H_{10}. Isomers may have different physical/chemical properties.

Chemistry review questions

Q1.　(C1, 2) Silicon is found in group 14 of the periodic table.

$$^{28}_{14}\text{Si}$$

Silicon-30 is an isotope of silicon. Which of the following statements is true for silicon-30?

A.　14 protons, 14 neutrons and 14 electrons.
B.　14 protons, 16 neutrons and 14 electrons.
C.　16 protons, 14 neutrons and 16 electrons.
D.　30 neutrons plus protons and 16 electrons.

Answer ☐

Q2. (C4a) An organic compound is combusted and found to contain 36 per cent carbon, 6 per cent hydrogen and 48 per cent oxygen by mass. Which of the following is the correct chemical formula of the compound?

A. $C_2H_4O_2$
B. $C_4H_{10}O$
C. $C_3H_6O_3$
D. $C_6H_{12}O_4$
E. $C_2H_2O_2$

(hint: take 100 g)

Answer ☐

Q3. (C4a) How many dm^3 (litres) of carbon dioxide are produced if 200 ml of 1.0 molar (1 M) hydrochloric acid is added to 0.5 moles of calcium carbonate? (1 mole of any gas occupies 24 dm^3 at RTP.)
$CaCO_3 + 2HCl = CaCl_2 + H_2O + CO_2$.

A. 24
B. 12
C. 2.4
D. 1.2

(hint: 1.0 M = 1 mol per litre)

Answer ☐

Q4. (C4b) The body burns glucose with oxygen to release energy. The end products are carbon dioxide and water. What values of a, b and c are needed to balance the equation?

$$C_6H_{12}O_6 + aO_2 = bCO_2 + cH_2O.$$

(hint: b first)

$a = \ldots$
$b = \ldots$
$c = \ldots$

Q5.   (C5ii) In which of the following compounds does carbon have the lowest oxidation number?

A. CF_4
B. CH_4
C. C_2H_6
D. CF_3
E. C

(hint: 0, –, +)

Answer [＿＿＿＿]

Q6.   (C4a) A dehydrated patient is prescribed 1.0 L Normal saline (9 g/L NaCl), given by subcutaneous infusion over eight hours. Which of the following calculations describes the number of millimoles of sodium infused? The AMU of sodium (atomic mass unit) is 23 and the AMU of chlorine is 35.5.

A. $9 \div (23 \div 58.5) \times 1000 = 6.7$ mmol
B. $9 \div 23 \times 1000 = 391.3$ mmol
C. $9 \div (23 \div 35.5) \times 1000 = 11.0$ mmol
D. $9 \div (23 + 35.5) \times 1000 = 153.8$ mmol

(hint: NaCl molecular mass)

Answer [＿＿＿＿]

Q7.   (C5ii) In photographic fixing, sodium thiosulphate removes unexposed silver bromide according to the following equation:

$$AgBr + 2[Na_2(S_2O_3)^{2-}] \longrightarrow Na_3[Ag(S_2O_3)_2]^{3-} + NaBr$$

Which of the following statements describes correctly the behaviour of the silver in the equation?

A. Ag is oxidized from +1 to +3 and acts as a reducing agent.
B. Ag is oxidized from +1 to +3 and acts as an oxidizing agent.
C. Ag is reduced from +1 to 0 and acts as an oxidizing agent.
D. Ag is oxidized from –1 to 0 and acts as a reducing agent.

(hint: Na cations)

Answer [＿＿＿＿]

Q8. (C5c, C6) Sulphur dioxide reacts with oxygen to produce sulphur trioxide according to the following equilibrium:

$$2SO_{2(g)} + O_{2(g)} = 2SO_{3(g)} \quad \Delta H = -390 \text{ kJ}.$$

Which one of the following changes moves the equilibrium most in favour of sulphur trioxide?

A. Increase temperature and increase pressure.
B. Increase temperature and increase reactant concentrations.
C. Increase temperature and add a catalyst.
D. Decrease temperature and add a catalyst.
E. Decrease temperature and increase pressure.

(hint: not rate)

Answer [   ]

Q9. (C6a,b) Which of the following aqueous solutions will have a pH of approximately 10?

A. 1 M sodium chloride.
B. 0.01 M hydrochloric acid.
C. 0.001 M sulphuric acid.
D. 0.001 M sodium hydroxide.
E. 0.0001 M potassium hydroxide.

(hint: $[H^+][OH^-] = 10^{-14}$)

Answer [   ]

Q10. (C9) The apparatus below shows the electrolysis of copper sulphate solution using carbon (inert) electrodes. Choose the correct term, substance or equation (labelled A to E) from the list below to match each label on the diagram (i to iv).

A = oxidation; B = reduction; $C = Cu^{2+} + 2e^- = Cu$; $D = O_2$; $E = Cl_2$.

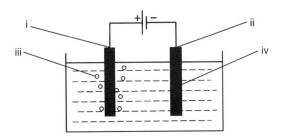

i) = ...
ii) = ...
iii) = ...
iv) = ...

Q11. (C9, P14a, P15) The graph shows the time–temperature curve of pure ice when heated.

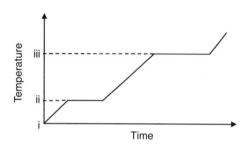

Which of the following statements are true and which are false?

A. There are three phases with two phase changes in between.
B. The temperature at i is 273 K.
C. Water is boiling between temperatures ii and iii.
D. The temperature at iii is 373 K.
E. The water temperature rises by 100 K between ii and iii.

Answer [   ]

Q12. (C10c) Choose the chemical formula (labelled A to I) from the list below to match each numbered space (i to v) in the following text. Some formulae are not used.

A = C_2H_6;   B = C_8H_{18};   C = $C_{10}H_{22}$;   D = CH_3OH;   E = $C_2H_4Br_2$;
F = HBr;   G = C_2H_4;   H = C_2H_5Br;   I = Br_2.

In cracking, [...i...] is broken down into [...ii...] and ethene [...iii...]. Ethene is unsaturated and it will react with [...iv...] to produce the colourless liquid 1,2-dibromoethane [...v...].

i) = ...
ii) = ...
iii) = ...
iv) = ...
v) = ...

5

Biology review

B1. Digestive system

a) *Passage of food*

Mouth, tongue, pharynx (throat), oesophagus (food pipe), stomach, small intestine (duodenum, ileum) and large intestine (colon, rectum).

b) *Nutrients and catalytic enzymes*

i)   Carbohydrates: (polysaccharides) digested with salivary amylase (to disaccharides (eg maltose) and monosaccharides (eg glucose)).

ii)   Proteins: digested with pepsin, trypsin and chymotrypsin in the stomach (to polypeptides and amino acids).

iii) Fats: digested with bile salts (emulsify/solubulize) and pancreatic amylase, trypsin and lipase (to fatty acids and glycerol). Most absorption of nutrients takes place in the small intestine via the blood capillaries of villi (large surface area).

Enzymes (protein molecules) are food specific and have an optimum pH (pH 2 in stomach; pH 7 in the mouth and small intestine; eg salivary amylase stops working in the stomach) and work best at body temperature (37 °C; denature above 45 °C). The digestive tract is lubricated with mucus, which protects it from the digestive enzymes. Water is absorbed by the large intestine and indigestible material is eliminated.

B2. Respiratory system

a) *Air pathway*

Nose, nasal cavity, pharynx (throat) larynx (voice box), trachea (windpipe), two bronchi (one bronchus enters each lung), bronchioles and alveoli.

b) *Respiration*

i) Breathing (pulmonary ventilation): the physical process of inspiration/expiration: on *inspiration* the diaphragm and intercostal muscles *contract*, the diaphragm moves down, the thoracic volume increases, the pressure decreases and air is drawn into the lungs. On *expiration* the muscles *relax*, the diaphragm moves upwards, the thoracic volume decreases, the thoracic pressure increases and the lungs deflate.

ii) External respiration: the exchange of oxygen and carbon dioxide in the lungs between the alveoli and the pulmonary capillaries. *Diffusion* of gases in the alveoli is aided by a large surface area, thin walls, moist lining and good blood supply. Oxygen is carried to respiring cells by red blood cells (RBCs); haemoglobin (Hb) in RBCs binds four molecules of oxygen as oxyhaemoglobin (HbO_8); carbon dioxide from respiring cells is carried away as hydrogen carbonate ions.

iii) Internal respiration: cellular respiration in the tissues that combines oxygen and glucose to produces adenosine triphosphate (ATP) energy for cellular process and carbon dioxide as a by-product. When the demand for oxygen exceeds the supply then *anaerobic* respiration can be used to generate ATP energy; lactic acid is the by-product.

B3. Circulatory system

a) *Heart and lungs*

Deoxygenated blood from the venous system reaches the *right atrium* of the heart from the body via the inferior and superior *vena cava*; it passes through the *tricuspid valve* (contains three cusps/flaps) into the *right ventricle* of the heart to be pumped out of the heart through the pulmonary *valve* (prevents backflow) via the *pulmonary arteries* (the only artery to carry de-oxygenated blood) to the lungs; oxygenated blood leaves the lungs via the *pulmonary veins* and reaches the *left atrium* of the heart, passing through the *bicuspid* (mitral) *valve* and into the *left ventricle* before being pumped out of the heart through the *aortic valve* into the *aorta* and to the body.

i) Direction of flow: blood flows from the right to the left side of the heart via the lungs to be oxygenated: right atrium; tricuspid valve; right ventricle; pulmonary valve; pulmonary arteries (de-oxygenated); lungs; pulmonary capillaries (carbon dioxide lost and oxygen gained) pulmonary veins (oxygenated); bicuspid (mitral) valve; left ventricle; aortic valve; aorta and systemic arteries.

ii) Order of valves (four) tricuspid, pulmonary, bicuspid (mitral), then aortic ('tricycle before bicycle').

iii) Heart beat: rate controlled by electrical impulses from the sinoatrial (SA) node (pacemaker cells in the wall of the right atrium); atria contract first followed by the ventricles (impulses from the atrioventricular (AV) node, the bundle of His (AV bundle) and the Purkinje fibres); in other words, both atria contract together followed by both ventricles together a fraction of a second later.

iv) Blood pressure: systolic over diastolic (eg 120/70): systole (heart contracts) and diastole (heart relaxes); systole + diastole = cardiac cycle (eg 75 cycles/min or one every 0.8 seconds).

v) Cardiac output (ml/min) = stroke volume (ml) × heart rate (beats per minute).

b) *Blood*

i) Composition: 55% = plasma (of which 90% = water; 7% = proteins); 45% = cells (99% = red; 1% = white).

ii) Functions: transports oxygen, carbon dioxide, nutrients, waste products and hormones and clotting factors (plasma); regulates pH, temperature and osmotic pressure (plasma proteins); protects: *leucocytes* (white blood cells) fight infection; *lymphocytes* (two types): helper T-cells that mature in the thymus gland and B-cells that mature in the bone marrow and produce antibodies that respond to antigens (foreign bodies).

B4. Nervous system; eye

a) *CNS and PNS*

The central nervous system (CNS) includes the brain and spinal cord but excludes the peripheral nervous system (PNS). Thirty-one pairs of spinal nerves (left and right) fan out from the spinal cord to form the PNS.

i) Nerve impulse path: sensory *receptor* stimulated (eg skin), nerve impulses (electrical messages) sent via a sensory (*afferent*) neurone (ascending pathway) of the peripheral nervous system (PNS) to the central nervous system (CNS) and then away (descending pathway) from the CNS via a motor (*efferent*) neurone (of the PNS) to an *effector* (muscle or gland).

ii) Reflex arc: sensory receptor neurone stimulated (eg hot surface); nerve impulse sent via an afferent neurone to a motor neurone via an *interneurone* (a relay neurone) in the spinal cord (the brain receives an impulse later). The *cerebral cortex* can override the reflex arc (eg not wishing to drop a valuable hot object).

b) *Autonomic (involuntary) nervous system (ANS)*

Controls the automatic functions of the body that maintain stable internal conditions (ie *homeostasis*) (eg respiration, heart rate, blood pressure, temperature and salt-water balance). The *hypothalamus* (of the brain) regulates many of the body's autonomic systems (eg temperature through vasodilation/constriction; the *pons* regulates breathing).

c) *The eye*

The iris (two sets of muscles) controls the amount of light entering the pupil by contracting the circular muscle (for bright light) or the radial muscle (in dim light); the dilation or constriction of the pupil is by autonomic reflex arc. Photoreceptors (light-sensitive rod and cone cells), contained in the retina, measure intensity, wavelength and position of light; impulses are relayed via ganglion cells to the optic nerve, which transmits impulses to the brain. The image on the retina is inverted and results from the refraction of light at the cornea with fine adjustment at the lens; the image is sharpest near to the centre of the retina at the *fovea*. The focus of the lens can be altered from infinity (parallel light) to a near object by the *accommodation* reflex (focus at a near object = maximum accom-modation = maximum curvature (more spherical)) (see also Physics P16f). The ciliary muscles are responsible for changing the shape of the lens: near object = ciliary muscles contract = suspensory ligaments loose = more convex lens (fatter) = more diffraction; distant object = ciliary muscles relaxed = suspensory ligaments taut = less convex lens (thinner) = less diffraction.

B5. Endocrine system; menstrual cycle hormones

a) *Endocrine glands*

Secrete *hormones* (chemical messengers) into the bloodstream; respond more slowly than the nervous system and the effects are longer-lasting.

i) Pineal gland (*melatonin*) and pituitary gland (eg *growth hormone*; *oxytocin* in child-birth); thyroid (eg *thyroxine* to increase the metabolic rate) and parathyroid glands (eg increase blood calcium); thymus gland (*thymosin* for T-lymphocytes in immunity).

ii) Pancreas (eg *insulin* to reduce blood glucose levels and *glucagon* to increase blood sugar levels).

iii) Adrenal glands (eg *steroid hormones* in response to stress); ovaries (*oestrogen* and *progesterone*) and testes (*testosterone*). The kidney is not an endocrine gland but it secretes the hormone *erythropoietin* (EPO) to increase red blood cell production.

b) *Negative feedback*

Resists change; inhibits any deviation from the *norm*. Detection of a change inhibits the change; for example, food intake = a rise in blood glucose above the norm is detected by receptors in the pancreas = insulin hormone secreted by the pancreas (beta cells) travels to the *target organ* = liver stores glucose as glycogen = drop in blood glucose level = pancreas detects the drop and stops producing insulin = normal glucose levels achieved. If the blood glucose level is too low, the pancreas detects this and secretes glucagons (alpha cells), stimulating the release of glucose by the liver. Most homeostatic controls use negative feedback mechanism to *oppose any change*.

c) *Positive feedback*

Magnifies change; promotes any deviation from the norm.

Detection of a change stimulates the change, eg start of menstrual cycle = rise in pituitary FSH (follicle-stimulating hormone) = ovaries produce more oestrogen = rise in pituitary LH (luteinizing hormone) = ovaries produce more oestrogen = LH surge. A positive feedback mechanism *magnifies any change*.

d) *Menstrual cycle hormones*

FSH level rises promoting the growth of ovarian follicles that release *oestrogen*, causing the *endometrium* to build to full thickness; LH (luteinizing hormone) peaks on mid-cycle (day 14) to stimulate ovulation, that is, the release of a matured *oocyte* (egg) from the follicle into the Fallopian tube; LH acts on the empty follicle to form the *corpus luteum*, which secretes oestrogen and progesterone; the latter rises to maintain gestation and inhibit FSH (prevents further ovulation). If the egg is not fertilized with a sperm (ie no *zygote*) then the corpus luteum breaks down. Both positive and negative feedback loops operate during the menstrual cycle.

B6. Urinary system

a) *Components*

Kidneys, ureters, urinary bladder and urethra.

b) *Kidney and nephron*

i) Kidney anatomy: renal cortex (outer), medulla (middle) and renal pelvis (inner) continuous with the ureter that leads into the bladder. *Nephrons* are the functional units of the kidney and extend from the cortex (glomerular filtration) into the medulla (filtrate re-absorption and urine concentration).

ii) Nephron: a schematic diagram of a nephron is shown below.

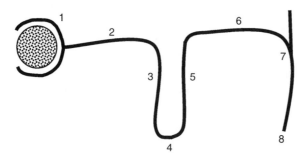

(1) *Renal corpuscle* = *Bowman's* capsule (glomerular capsule) + *glomerulus* (bundle of capillaries) attached to (2) the *proximal convoluted* (coiled) *tubule*, which leads into (3) the descending limb of (4) the *loop of Henle* (nephron loop or medullary loop), leading to (5) the ascending limb extending to (6) the *distal convoluted tubule* emptying into (7) the collecting duct and (8) the renal pelvis.

c) *Filtration and selective re-absorption*

1 = *Protein* not filtered out and remains in the blood.

2 = 100 per cent of *glucose* re-absorbed back into the blood capillaries; two-thirds of *sodium* (salt) and *water* re-absorbed.

3 = Only water is re-absorbed and not sodium.

4 = Sodium concentration is at its highest.

5 = Only sodium re-absorbed (eg pumped out when *aldosterone* is released by the endocrine gland on the top of each kidney).

6 = More sodium reabsorbed.

7 = If dehydrated (high *osmotic pressure*/solutes) antidiuretic hormone (ADH) is released by the pituitary gland and water is re-absorbed, otherwise urine remains dilute.

8 = Waste products excreted in urine: *urea* (50% of it) and creatinine (100% of it).

d) *Blood flow*

Aorta, renal artery, arteries of kidney; afferent arterioles to glomerulus capillaries; efferent arteriole from glomerulus to network of blood capillaries surrounding nephrons; veins of kidney, renal vein and inferior vena cava.

B7. DNA (deoxyribonucleic acid), genes and cell division

a) *Genes*

The nucleus of human cells contains 46 chromosomes (22 pairs and two sex chromosomes). Each chromosome contains thousands of genes made up of chains of DNA nucleotides. The nucleotides consist of a sugar molecule (deoxyribose), a phosphate group and one of four possible nitrogenous 'base pairs': adenine (A), cytosine (C), guanine (G) and thymine (T). Each rung in the DNA double-stranded helix ladder is an A to T or C to G base pair.

b) *Gametes, somatic cells and the cell cycle*

i)   Gametes: diploid egg and sperm cells precursor cells divide by meiosis to produce male and female haploid *gametes* with nuclei that contain 23 chromosomes. These fuse during egg fertilization to produce a new cell, the *zygote,* which has a single diploid nucleus. During meiosis, diploid cells divide twice: once to give two diploid cells (DNA duplicated) and then once more to give four different haploid cells, each with a single copy of each chromosome (creates genetic variability); after fertilization the diploid chromosome number is restored. Only haploid cells, produced by meiosis and containing half the number of chromosomes, are suitable to become gametes.

ii) Somatic cells: these are non-sex cells that replicate by mitosis to produce two identical, diploid daughter cells with the same number of chromosomes as all the other somatic cells, including the zygote from which they originate.

iii) Cell cycle: cell growth and DNA replication (*interphase*) is followed by mitosis in four phases: *prophase (*chromosomes visible in nucleus and nuclear membrane dissolves), *metaphase* (line up along equator)*, anaphase* (chromosomes move apart) and finally *telophase* (nuclear membranes form and the cell divides in two).

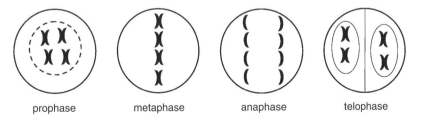

prophase	metaphase	anaphase	telophase

In other words, a cell can divide mitotically once it has two complete copies of its DNA (two copies from the father and two copies from the mother = ie $46 \times 2 = 92$ chromosomes after prophase).

B8. Patterns of inheritance

B8. *Inheritance (part 1)*

a) Punnett square

This shows all the possible combination of *alleles* derived from each parent; they can be either dominant (common) or recessive (rare); two alleles = one *genotype* (the DNA gentic code). The *phenotype* (trait) is the physical characteristic (eg brown eyes or blue eyes) expressed from the genotype. Thus: cells = nuclei = DNA = genes = alleles = genotypes = phenotypes (inherited *trait*).

b) Homozygous and heterozygous

i)   Two alleles the same = *homozygous* genotype; two different alleles = *heterozygous* genotype.

ii) Dominant and recessive: two dominant alleles = *homozygous dominant*; two recessive alleles = *homozygous recessive.* One dominant allele and one recessive allele = *heterozygous* dominant (recessive allele is masked by the dominant one).

c) Inherited abnormalities/disease

Autosomal (22 matching pairs of non-sex chromosomes or autosomes) and *X-linked* (1 pair of sex chromosomes X and Y).

i) **Autosomal dominant:** abnormality is in the dominant allele, eg Huntington's.
   If D = dominant trait (abnormality), d = recessive trait (normal) then heterozygous (Dd) will be abnormal; homozygous for the affected allele (DD) will be abnormal; homozygous for the normal allele (dd) will be normal. *Dominant genes (whether homozygous or heterozygous) always express the phenotype (= abnormality).*
   Punnett squares: one homozygous affected parent (DD) = 100% affected children (all Dd); one heterozygous affected parent (Dd) = 50% affected children (50/50 Dd/dd). Punnett squares = DD × dd = Dd, Dd, Dd, Dd (100%) and Dd × dd = Dd, Dd, dd, dd (50/50) respectively.

ii) **Autosomal recessive:** abnormality is in the recessive allele, eg cystic fibrosis.
   If N = dominant trait (normal); n = recessive trait (genetic disease/abnormality), then heterozygous child (Nn) will be normal but a *carrier* for the affected gene; homozygous child for the normal allele (NN) will be normal; homozygous child for the affected allele (nn) will be abnormal. *Recessive genes must be homozygous if they are expressed in the phenotype; if heterozygous, a carrier.*
   Punnett squares: one homozygous affected parent (nn) × one homozygous unaffected parent (NN) = 100% of children are carriers (all Nn); one homozygous affected parent (nn) × one heterozygous unaffected parent (Nn; *carrier*) = 50% of children are carriers (Nn) and 50% affected (nn); two heterozygous parents (both Nn) = 50% carriers (Nn), 25% affected (nn), 25% unaffected (NN).

Punnett squares = Nn, Nn, Nn, Nn (100%) and Nn, Nn, nn, nn (50/50). In the case of Nn, Nn, nn, NN (50/25/25), then in children not expressing the phenotype (ie Nn, Nn, NN), the probability of being a carrier (Nn) is two-thirds and the probability of not being a carrier (NN) is one-third.

B8. *Inheritance (part 2)*

iii) **X-linked inheritance:** abnormality/disease is caused by genes located on the X-chromosome; examples include haemophilia and colour blindness. Males are XY and females are XX. A male must pass his Y-gene on to his sons and his X-gene on to his daughters, so if he has the disease then all his daughters will inherit the affected gene but none of his sons. Affected females have a 50% chance that each son and each daughter will inherit the affected gene.

X-linked recessive X^a (most common): an affected male cannot have X-affected sons but his daughters are all carriers (they have a 'working copy' of the X-gene and do not develop the condition); female carriers have a 50% chance of a son being affected and a 50% chance of a daughter being a carrier. *X-linked abnormalities are passed on by female carriers and by affected males.*

X-linked dominant X^A (rare): affected male cannot have any X-affected sons (as per recessive) but his daughters are all affected; affected females have a 50% chance of a son being affected and a 50% chance of a daughter being affected (ie not a carrier). *If an affected male has an affected mother then she must be dominant for the trait; if the mother is not affected then she must be a carrier.*

d) Pedigree chart

Shows the genetic history of a family (eg grandparents, parents, children), that is, the inherited phenotypes. General patterns are as follows:

i)   Mostly males affected = X-linked abnormality.

ii) Males and females affected equally = autosomal.

iii) Every generation affected = dominant for the abnormality.

iv) Skips one or more generations = recessive for the abnormality.

For example, three generations: unaffected grandfather/grandmother with one married, affected son, one unaffected son, two unaffected daughters, one with affected sons.

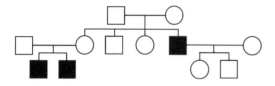

Key: male □ ; female ○ ; affected = shaded

X-linked recessive inheritance
(female carriers (heterozygous $X^A X^B$); males cannot pass on the trait to their sons)

B8. *Inheritance (part 3)*

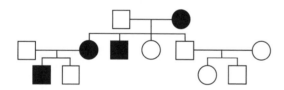

X-linked dominant inheritance
(affected males have affected mother)

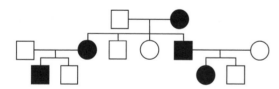

autosomal dominant inheritance
(50% of males and 50% of females affected in every generation with one affected parent (heterozygous))

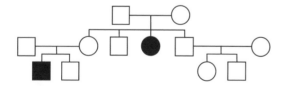

autosomal recessive
(25% of the children of unaffected parents (heterozygous) will express the recessive trait (homozygous))

Biology review questions

Q1. (B8(1)) If two heterozygous, phenotypically tall plants with a recessive gene for height are cross-pollinated, what will be the ratio of tall plants to short in the offspring?

A. 1:1
B. 1:2
C. 2:1
D. 3:1
E. 4:1

Answer

Q2. (B8(3)) If A = dominant abnormal trait, a = recessive normal trait, B = dominant normal trait and b = recessive abnormal trait, then what genotypes are expressed in the following pedigree?

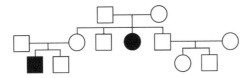

Key: male □ ; female ○ ; affected = shaded

Autosomal recessive (25% of the children of unaffected parents (heterozygous) will express the recessive trait (homozygous))

A. aa, Bb
B. Bb, bb
C. Bb, Bb
D. BB, Bb

Answer

Q3. (B8(3)) If A = dominant abnormal trait, a = recessive normal trait, B = dominant normal trait and b = recessive abnormal trait, then what genotypes are expressed in the following pedigree?

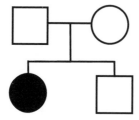

A. AA, Aa, aa
B. AA, aa
C. Aa, Aa
D. AA, aa, bb

Answer [   ]

Q4. (B4) Choose the correct word or term (labelled A to K) from the list below to match each numbered space (i to vii) in the text below. Some words or terms may be used more than once or not at all.
A = ascending; B = constrict; C = close; D = distant; E = autonomic; F = ciliary; G = rods and cones; H = convex; I = concave; J = optic nerve; K = efferent.

The iris of the eye acts as its aperture and is a good example of an [...i...] reflex. Light enters via the pupil and stimulates the [...ii...] in the retina. Impulses are sent to the central nervous system via the [...iii...]. The oculomotor nerve in the [...iv...] limb of the reflex arc innervates the muscles of the iris, controlling the size of the pupil. In the 'accommodation' reflex the [...v...] muscles adjust the focus of the lens. Long-sighted people can only see [...vi...] objects clearly and need glasses with a [...vii...] lens to refract the light more.

i = ...
ii = ...
iii = ...
iv = ...
v = ...
vi = ...
vii = ...

Q5. (B5c,d) In the menstrual cycle, which hormone peaks to trigger ovulation and which hormone peaks after ovulation has taken place?

   A. Oestrogen followed by progesterone.
   B. Follicle-stimulating hormone followed by progesterone.
   C. Luteinizing hormone followed by progesterone.
   D. Follicle-stimulating hormone followed by luteinizing hormone.
   E. Luteinizing hormone followed by oestrogen.

Answer ☐

Q6. (B1) Most of the chemical digestion of carbohydrates, protein and fats takes place in which part of the gastro-intestinal tract catalysed by enzymes released by which gland(s)?

   A. Stomach and thyroid gland.
   B. Stomach and pancreas gland.
   C. Duodenum and adrenal glands.
   D. Small intestine and pancreas gland.
   E. Small intestine and pituitary gland.

Answer ☐

Q7. (B8(1)) In the Punnett square shown below, 'A' is the dominant allele and 'a' is the recessive allele. How many genotypes are there and how many phenotypes are there?

	A	a
A	AA	Aa
a	Aa	aa

   A. 2 genotypes and 2 phenotypes.
   B. 3 genotypes and 2 phenotypes.
   C. 2 genotypes and 3 phenotypes.
   D. 3 genotypes and 3 phenotypes.
   E. 3 genotypes and 4 phenotypes.

Answer ☐

Q8.   (B2b, 3a) Red blood cells (RBCs) in the pulmonary artery contain:

    A. Less carbon dioxide than RBCs in the pulmonary vein and no oxygen.
    B. Less oxygen than RBCs in the pulmonary vein and no carbon dioxide.
    C. Less oxygen and less carbon dioxide than RBCs in the pulmonary vein.
    D. More oxygen and more carbon dioxide than RBCs in the pulmonary vein.
    E. Less oxygen and more carbon dioxide than RBCs in the pulmonary vein.

Answer ☐

Q9.   (B6) Which of the following substances are not found in the glomerular filtrate of a healthy kidney nephron?

1: urea; 2: glucose; 3: protein; 4: water; 5: sodium; 6: red blood cells.

    A. 1, 2, 4 and 5
    B. 2, 4 and 5
    C. 3 and 6
    D. 1 and 3
    E. 2, 3 and 6

6

Writing task review

In the BMAT writing task you have to answer one question out of the three choices available. The questions typically relate to philosophical or socio-cultural issues, which may favour candidates with an A level in the humanities. There is a time limit of 30 minutes and you can write no more than one A4 side of text, or about 300 words. If your handwriting is small or condensed you might exceed 350 words but if it is large or spaced out then you might only manage 270. Either way, most people, writing a minimum speed of 20 words per minute, will be able to write their answer in under 15 minutes, leaving 10 minutes to prepare the essay with a few minutes to check through it at the end.

W1. Choice of question (1 minute)

Read through *all* three questions quickly but carefully before making a decision. Grade each question after you have read it. If you like the question then give it a tick; if you are uncertain but it seems possible then give it a question mark; if it is definitely not the question for you then give it a cross. Do not assume automatically that the question you have ticked is the best choice. Look again at the more challenging question; it may offer the better-prepared candidate the chance to excel. NB: before you make your final decision, make sure that you can see *both sides of the argument*.

W2. Preparation (10 minutes)

Thorough planning is an essential part of your answer. It needs a beginning, middle and an end that cover all parts of the question. This hints at three paragraphs; however, an additional paragraph at the start serves as an introduction when the questions ask you explain what you think the author means or is trying to imply.

i) **Paragraphs:** each paragraph informs the examiner that you are covering a new aspect of the question, and each sentence in the paragraph carries a single idea related to the theme of the paragraph.

ii) **Sentences:** your sentences can (and should) vary in length from the short, for example 15 words or less, to the long, for example 26 words or more. Shorter sentences are easy to read and understand but if there are too many they make your work sound choppy and your ideas fragmented. Longer sentences make your ideas sound *unified* but they are more difficult to read and if a sentence carries too much detail the meaning becomes obscure. By way of example, the sentences on this page average 24 words.

iii) **Layout:** taking an average sentence length of 24 words, then you will need to write about 13 sentences in four paragraphs. By way of example, you could use a 2,3,4,4-sentence plan, consisting of two sentences for the introduction; three arguments that support the statement, including one example; four arguments that counter it, including one example; followed by a four-sentence conclusion.

W3. The four-paragraph approach (10 minutes preparation)

Four paragraphs: introduction, arguments for, arguments against and conclusion. Each paragraph relates to one aspect of this approach.

i) **First paragraph** (eg two sentences): at the preparatory stage you need to *identify the task* and jot down what it entails. The introduction usually involves paraphrasing, that is, re-stating in *your own words* what the question is asking or what points the author is trying to make. If the question contains a hidden assumption (see section A1b) then you may wish to highlight it here, but not to excess. Explain what the statement means to you in two or three sentences at most.

ii) **Second and third paragraphs:** use *brainstorming* as a first step to generate any ideas without judging their value; it is the quantity rather than the quality of the ideas that matters at this stage. Even so, it is worth classifying the ideas as either for or against the argument. You can do this by placing key words or phrases in two opposing columns, for or against the argument/statement.

FOR (eg choose your three best ideas in support of the argument)	AGAINST (eg choose your four best ideas counter to the argument)
Hints and tips when choosing ideas:	Hints and tips when choosing ideas:
• Avoid including too many examples; one may suffice. An example is not a substitute for a well-crafted argument. • Do not leave your best ideas until the last in an attempt to build a crescendo. Get to the heart of the matter straight away; you have 20 minutes. • Use arrows to link brainstorming ideas that are counter to each other.	• Avoid including too many examples; one or two examples that counter the argument may suffice. • Do not get drawn into an emotional response even if you disagree strongly with what is being asserted. Be dispassionate; do not set yourself against the argument. Maintain a balanced view and avoid unnecessary bias.

iii) **Fourth paragraph:** *Evaluate and synthesize* your arguments (discuss strengths and weaknesses) to formulate a coherent conclusion that takes a clear position or reconciles the differences (you can introduce your own opinions).

W4. Composing the essay (15 minutes)

Points to remember:

i) Do not deviate from your chosen topic and answer all the components. Make a confident start, for example:
 – 'I believe that the statement implies that…'
 – 'The statement argues that…'
 – 'The author makes the point that…'

ii) Remember to keep your handwriting legible.

iii) Be careful with your grammar, spelling and syntax to avoid losing marks.

Avoid jargon or abbreviations. If you were to use the word 'cerebrovascular accident', put CVA in brackets after it; now you can use CVA if you need it again. Alternatively you could use the word 'stroke' as no special technical knowledge is expected.

iv) Follow your plan, keeping to one theme per paragraph; use linking words and phrases to facilitate a smooth transition from one paragraph to the next and to inform the examiner that you are starting a new theme, for example:
 – 'On the other hand…'
 – 'To counter these assertions…'
 – 'However, it might also be said…'

v) Vary the length of your sentences whilst keeping to one idea per sentence; short sentences make your work easier to understand.

vi) Use bullet points or roman numerals to make sequential points clearly (as in this list) but you must write a *unified* essay.

vii) The final paragraph: here you can take a clear position as long as you have weighed up the arguments for and against to reach and informed decision.

W5. The final check (2–3 minutes)

Spend a few minutes reading through your essay to check your punctuation, spelling and grammar, and to spot any missed-out words. Have you avoided repetition? Does it flow with good transitions between paragraphs? Remember your answer must not exceed a single side of A4 paper.

Example essay 1. Patients should not be offered choices in their medical treatment; doctors know what is best for them.

What does the author mean by this statement? Develop a counter-argument. Do you believe that patients should be allowed to choose their own treatments?

For	Against
1. Patient expects doctor to find a cure.	1. Patient autonomy; the right to choose.
2. Doctor more knowledgeable, also impartial/objective.	2. Patient not involved = poor self-care, eg diabetes.
3. Doctor knows the best treatment options.	3. Doctor's choice may not suit the individual's needs.
	4. Doctor takes all of the responsibility.

Essay 1

The author believes that doctors are the best people to make decisions about a patient's treatment.[1] The statement implies that patients can be excluded from the decision-making process.[2]

Whilst the author's view is very one-sided, it is true that patients look to their doctor to diagnose health problems and offer curative treatments [*supports argument*].[3] Furthermore, [*more support*] patients may lack the necessary knowledge to make decisions about their treatment and are not best placed to view their health problems impartially or dispassionately.[4]

However [*against*], it is not appropriate for a doctor to dictate to a patient what should and should not be done to the patient's own body.[5] This would be ethically unsound as it detracts from freedom of choice and might infringe upon the patient's human rights.[6] In addition [*also against*], unless the patient is involved in the decision-making process, the outcome of the treatment may not meet with the patient's lifestyle needs.[7] For example, [*one only*] failure to discuss treatments for diabetes may lead to poor patient practices in blood sugar control; errors in self-injecting insulin, for example, could be dangerous.[8] Furthermore, [*against again*] should a treatment fail, the patient will blame the doctor for the poor outcome and will not share any of the responsibility.[9]

Although it is beneficial for patients to be included in the decision-making process, this is not to say that they should dictate their treatments [*last part of question*].[10] The NHS is a rationed service that has to meet the needs of patients fairly within the resources available.[11] Thus [*reconciling*], whilst some patients may wish to remain as passive recipients in their medical treatment, ideally all patients should be included in the decision-making process.[12] The doctor should discuss the treatment options with the patient to facilitate joint decisions that satisfy both parties.[13]

The following example essay also uses a four-paragraph approach but does so in a different way. The arguments supporting the statement flow naturally from the introduction and an additional paragraph is used to answer the second part of the question.

Example essay 2. Mental health has nothing to do with physical well-being.

What do you take this statement to mean? Develop a counter-argument that refutes the author's view. Do you believe that a healthy mind equals a healthy body?

For	Against
1. Can be physically healthy and mentally ill at same time.	1. Mental illness: loss of motivation to maintain health; self-neglect.
2. Psychiatric medicine is a distinct branch of medicine.	2. Illness = physical stress = mental stress = mental stress
3. Physical ailments do not lead to mental health problems.	3. Pain; anxiety; eg heart attack leads to depression.
	4. Positive mental attitude is good for recovery.

Essay 2

The statement implies that there is no synergy between the mind and the body where mental and physical health is concerned. It also suggests that mental illness cannot be blamed on a lack of physical health. The fact that the treatment of psychiatric problems is a separate branch of medicine may lend support to this view. Furthermore, [*more support*] it is certainly the case that a person can be mentally ill yet physically healthy at the same time.

However, [*against*] people who suffer from mental health problems may be less motivated to maintain their physical health or may lack the capacity to do so. For example, [*first one*] lack of mental health can detract from physical health when a person fails to hold down a job and a lack of money leads to a poor diet or bad housing. More directly, [*second example*] stress and anxiety can lead to a rise in blood pressure, which increases the risk of heart disease and stroke; physical illness and the experience of hospitalization can be highly stressful.

Whilst it may be difficult to show empirically [*measure*] that a healthy mind equals a healthy body, [*second part of question*] people with a positive outlook on life are more likely to adopt healthier lifestyles. It is generally accepted that a positive mental attitude towards physical illness speeds recovery. By way of example, the prevention of depression in heart attack patients increases their chances of regaining health and reduces mortality.

It is clear that the experience of physical illness and the failure to cope with it can be detrimental to mental health and that mental health problems can, either directly or indirectly, impair physical health. However, [*reconciling*] it is also true that a healthy body does not guarantee a healthy mind any more than a healthy mind can guarantee a healthy body.

Instructions for mock tests

The following tests should be attempted under exam conditions as per the BMAT: that is, in the allotted time and without a calculator or dictionary. These are full mock tests and provide the equivalent of three BMAT tests (nine papers). Candidates will find some questions easier than others, depending upon their chosen college subjects.

Almost every question comes with its revision topics shown in parentheses. For example (P3b; M6d) means revise Physics topic 3b and Maths topic 6d; (B1a; C10b,c) means revise Biology topic 1a and Chemistry topics 10b and 10c. The mock tests in this book are regarded as part of the learning process, and for this reason some questions include a helpful hint as to the method of solution. These hints encourage you to have a go rather than to jump to the answer if you feel you cannot do it. However, candidates should try to answer the question without referring to the hint in the first instance.

BMAT SECTION 1 (Mock tests 1, 4 and 7): Aptitude and skills

You have 35 questions to answer in one hour. Calculators are not permitted. Record your answers on a separate sheet of paper.

BMAT SECTION 2 (Mock tests 2, 5 and 8): Scientific knowledge and applications

You have 30 minutes to answer 27 questions. Calculators are not permitted. Record your answers on a separate sheet of paper.

BMAT SECTION 3 (Mock test 3, 6 and 9): Writing task

You have 30 minutes to write a unified essay on one of the questions. Your answer must be contained on a single side of A4 paper (30 lines). Dictionaries are not permitted.

Part 2

Tests and answers

7

Mock tests

Section 1 Aptitude and skills

Mock test 1

35 questions
Time allowed one hour
No calculators

Q1. (A2, 3) Motorway speed limits should no longer be restricted to 70 mph. More than half of all motorists admit to driving at 80 mph or above so it may as well be made legal. Driving at 10 mph above the current limit is not frowned upon and few drivers believe that they will be prosecuted for doing so.

Which of the following best expresses the main point of the passage?

A. It is as safe to drive at 80 mph as it is at 70 mph.
B. Most drivers are quite happy to disobey speed limits.
C. Drivers frequently exceed 80 mph on motorways.
D. Driving at 80 mph on motorways is accepted behaviour.
E. Cars can be driven at 80 mph without fear of prosecution.

Answer [   ]

Q2. (A2, 3) Non-smokers should take priority over smokers where NHS treatment is concerned. People who engage in smoking are responsible for their own health problems. Those people who have made efforts to maintain their health should not have to wait for treatment behind smokers who have ignored it.

Statement: If all the non-smokers who failed to exercise, watch their weight or avoid excessive alcohol consumption went to the back of the queue there would be few people left at the front.

Which of the following best describes how the short statement relates to the argument?

A. It lends significant support to the argument.
B. It presents a significant challenge to the argument.
C. It restates the conclusion of the argument.
D. It restates one of the premises of the argument.
E. It neither supports nor challenges the argument.

Answer [   ]

Q3. (A2, 3) Nuclear power provides cheap and clean electricity. Almost 80 per cent of the electricity needs of France are met by nuclear power plants compared to a paltry 20 per cent in the UK. Coal-fired power stations produce 50 times more carbon dioxide per kilowatt-hour than do nuclear power plants, and fossil fuels will eventually run out. The government should support a new generation of nuclear power stations to tackle climate change and ensure sustainable energy supplies in the future. The UK lags behind France in nuclear technology so the power stations will have to be built and run by French companies.

Which one of the following, if true, would most seriously weaken the above argument?

A. The UK has a better spread of energy sources than France and can look towards 'renewables' for additional power.
B. The UK will lose its independence in power generation if nuclear power stations dominate energy sources.
C. The construction and decommissioning of nuclear reactors are expensive, and have a large carbon footprint.
D. Cutting back on energy consumption would reduce carbon dioxide emissions without the risks from nuclear power.
E. France's lack of natural resources meant that it had to embrace nuclear power.

Answer [   ]

Q4. (M9a) What fraction of the square is shaded if A and C are the mid-points of the two sides?

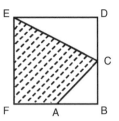

Answer [   ]

Q5. (M13b) The bar chart compares the hospital admissions for asthma per 100 000 population, for children in selected European countries. There are 12 million children in the UK and 10 million in Spain. How many children in the UK have been admitted to hospital with asthma?

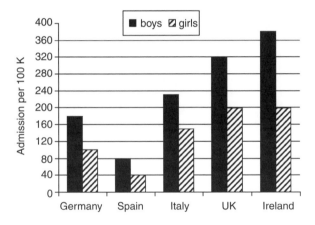

A. 24 000
B. 32 000
C. 52 000
D. 62 400
E. 84 000

Answer [   ]

Q6. (M13b) What is the difference between the UK and Spain in the number of hospital admissions for boys?

    A. 24 000
    B. 22 400
    C. 30 400
    D. 20 000
    E. 32 000

Answer [ ]

Q7. (M4b) What is the boy-to-girl ratio of hospital admissions in the UK, assuming the UK has an equal population of male and female children?

    A. 8:5
    B. 1:1.6
    C. 4:3
    D. 1:1
    E. 3:2

Answer [ ]

Q8. (M4b) Which country had the highest ratio of boys to girls, assuming each country has an equal population of male and female children?

    A. Germany.
    B. Spain.
    C. Italy.
    D. UK.
    E. Ireland.

Answer [ ]

Q9.   (A) Which shape comes next in the following sequence of shapes?

Answer [   ]

Q10. (A2, 3) Wind farms are a poor source of power. When the wind stops blowing, not a single watt of power is produced.

Which of the following is an implicit assumption of the above argument?

A.   The wind must blow continuously for power to be produced.
B.   Lack of wind makes wind farms an unreliable power source.
C.   Wind farms can only produce power intermittently.
D.   Wind farms are an expensive means of producing power.
E.   Failure to produce power makes wind farms a poor power source.

Answer [   ]

Q11. (A2, 3) Cellulitis is a bacterial skin infection that mainly affects the extremities. It can be treated with anti-microbial therapy directed by blood culture and antibiotic sensitivity results. However, contamination by other bacteria on the skin usually leads to a high proportion of false positives.

Which of the following can safely be inferred from the above paragraph?

A.   It is best to wait for the results of a blood culture and sensitivity test before initiating anti-microbial therapy.
B.   Cellulitis will only respond to one antibiotic.
C.   Bacterial contamination leads to a low proportion of false negatives.
D.   The taking of blood cultures is often of no help in directing the treatment of cellulitis.
E.   Cases of cellulitis are restricted to the arms and legs.

Answer [   ]

Q12. Place the following four sentences in the order in which they form the most coherent passage.

A. Deep sea organisms do not replenish their carbon from the air so they contain a higher proportion of inactive carbon.

B. Carbon-14 dating is not an infallible method of determining the age of ancient artefacts and organic matter.

C. Consequently they can have an anomalous carbon-dating age that appears much older than the true age.

D. It works best on once-living remains that consumed carbon from the air where the carbon-14 to carbon-12 ratio is fixed.

Answer [   ]

Q13. (A2, 3) In order to cause an infection, pathogenic bacteria must find a host. Therefore, if pathogenic bacteria find a host they will cause an infection.

To which one of the following criticisms is the above argument vulnerable?

A. It assumes that all pathogenic bacteria will find a host.

B. It assumes that finding a host is sufficient for pathogenic bacteria to cause an infection.

C. It assumes that pathogenic bacteria cause infections.

D. It assumes that after finding a host there is a high probability that the pathogenic bacteria will cause an infection.

E. It assumes that pathogenic bacteria require a host to cause an infection.

Answer [   ]

Q14. (A2, 3) Cannabis should be legalized for both recreational and medicinal use. Marijuana is not considered addictive and smoking a 'joint' or 'reefer' is no different from smoking tobacco; its effects are similar to that of alcohol intoxication without the tendency for antisocial behaviour. Furthermore, the many and varied medical benefits of cannabis are well known. For example, the medical profession acknowledges that cannabis can relieve the symptoms of multiple sclerosis (MS). Therefore, the main reason for not legalizing cannabis must be the moral judgement that all drugs are bad; cannabis is a drug so cannabis is bad.

Which of the following is an unstated assumption of the above argument?

A. Cannabis is less addictive than tobacco.
B. Alcohol can lead to antisocial behaviour, unlike cannabis.
C. Like all drugs, cannabis is bad.
D. Cannabis use in MS is supported by the medical profession.
E. There is no difference between recreational and medicinal use.

Answer ☐

Q15. (M2e) Find the two missing numbers in the following series.

0, 1, 1, 2, 3, 5, ?, ?, 21, 34.

Answer: ☐

Q16. (M9) The diagram shows a square wedding cake iced on all sides excluding the base. It measures 30 cm × 30 cm × 15 cm deep. It is to be cut into identical portions measuring 5 cm × 5 cm × 5 cm. How many portions will have icing on them?

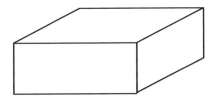

A. 90
B. 76
C. 60
D. 48
E. 40

(hint: 3 layers)

Answer ☐

Q17. (M7b) A wholesaler buys a book from a publisher with a discount of 50 per cent off the retail price. The wholesaler marks the book up 40 per cent for the bookshop. What percentage does the bookseller add on to reach retail price? Give your answer to the nearest whole number.

Answer ☐

Q18. (P5) The graph shows the speed of a train passing five stations: H, I, J, K and L.

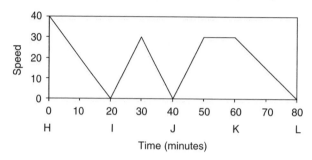

Which two pairs of stations are the same distances apart?

A. HI and JK.
B. HI and KL.
C. IJ and KL.
D. IJ and JK.
E. HJ and JL.

Answer ☐

Q19. If six guests at a dinner party all shake hands with each other, how many hand-shakes will there be?

A. 16
B. 15
C. 14
D. 12
E. 10

(hint: hexagon)

Answer ☐

Q20. (M13a) The pie charts show the distribution of A-level grades in two different schools, X and Y.

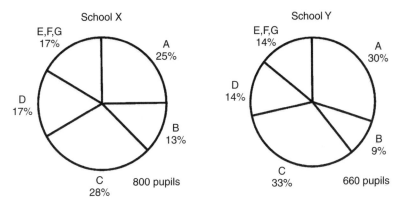

Which of the following can be deduced from the pie charts?

1. School X achieved more A-grades at A level than School Y.
2. The number of pupils achieving grade C or above in School X is 528.
3. The A–C pass rate in School Y was 5 per cent above that in School X.

A. 1 and 2.
B. 2 and 3.
C. 1 and 3.
D. All.
E. None.

Answer [ ]

Q21. (A2, 3) People on low incomes cannot afford to eat a healthy diet. Instead they eat high-fat snack foods like chocolate, which contains more calories per unit cost than fresh fruit and vegetables.

Which of the following is the best statement of the flaw in the above argument?

A. Most people on low incomes are not undernourished.
B. Chocolate contains more calories but it is less satiating than fresh foods.
C. Meals containing fresh fruit and vegetable take too long to prepare in comparison with snack foods.
D. Most people on low incomes count cost but not calories when choosing food.

Answer [ ]

Q22. (A2, 3) Today, medical paternalism has given way to patient autonomy. This means that each individual has the right to accept, choose or refuse a treatment based on what each believes to be in his or her own best interests. Failure to consent to a life-saving treatment no longer implies that the patient is incapable of making the 'right decision'. Doctors have a duty to ensure that patients are able to make an informed choice, including why one course of treatment might be the preferred option, but they cannot exert any pressure beyond that of 'gentle persuasion'.

Which of the following best summarizes the passage?

A. The doctor should assist a patient in making decisions that are consistent with the patient's own beliefs and values.
B. The patient's viewpoint is the only one that is important when deciding upon a medical treatment.
C. The doctor must respect the patient's wishes at all times even when the patient's life is at risk.
D. The doctor must act in the patient's best interests by identifying the preferred treatment option.

Answer [   ]

Q23. (A2, 3). Pensioners account for one-fifth of the population and will need 75 per cent of their former earnings, amounting to 15 per cent of gross domestic product (GDP), if they are to avoid a sharp decline in living standards. The state pension amounts to a paltry 4 per cent of GDP and private pensions can barely match this meagre amount, leaving a large gap. Clearly many people of retirement age are going to find it hard to make ends meet in the future.

Which two of the following show that the conclusion is unsafe even if the evidence is correct?

A. It might be the case that many people of retirement age will choose to carry on working to make up the gap.
B. It might be that in the future GDP will increase, which means that pensions will also rise.
C. It might be the case that the stock market will improve and income from private pensions will increase twofold.
D. It might be the case that many pensioners will make ends meet on less than three-quarters of their former earnings.

Answer [   ]

Q24. (M13e) The table shows the percentage of females with a cardiovascular-related condition, by age and diagnosis.

Diagnosis/Age	25–34	35–44	45–54	55–64	65–74	75+
Angina	0.0	0.2	1.3	3.1	6.3	9.1
Heart murmur	1.0	0.9	1.2	1.4	1.8	2.2
Arrhythmia	1.0	1.5	2.2	2.5	3.3	4.2
Myocardial infarction	0.0	0.2	0.3	0.6	0.7	1.7
Stroke	0.1	0.1	0.1	0.3	0.4	1.8
Diabetes	0.3	0.9	1.5	2.5	4.8	5.3
Hypertension	1.5	3.7	7.8	20.5	27.9	26.8

Which conditions show more than a 500 per cent increase in prevalence between the age ranges of 45–54 and 75+?

A. Angina only.
B. Angina and myocardial infarction.
C. Angina, myocardial infarction and diabetes.
D. Angina, myocardial infarction and hypertension.
E. Angina, myocardial infarction and stroke.

Answer ▢

Q25. (M12a.iv) The incidence of which conditions varies the least with age?

Answer ▢

Q26. (A4b) If most members of a ramblers' group are members of a hikers' group and a few of the hikers are members of a climbers' group, then which of the following statements must be true?

1. Most members of the climbers' group are not ramblers.
2. Most members of the hikers' group are ramblers.
3. No members belong to all three groups.

A. 1 only.
B. 2 only.
C. 3 only.
D. 1 and 2 only.
E. none.

(hint: three-circle problem, C,R,H, left to right)

Answer ▢

Q27. (A2) Consider the following two statements and the conclusion that follows:

i)   Aptitude tests are a reliable predictor of degree performance (*major premise*).
ii) The BMAT is an aptitude test (*minor premise*).
iii) The BMAT is a reliable predictor of degree performance (*conclusion*).

Which one of the following is invalid?

A. If i) is false then iii) is unsafe.
B. If ii) is false then iii) is unsafe.
C. If iii) is true then i) and ii) are true.
D. If iii) is unsafe then i) and/or ii) are false.
E. If i) and ii) are true then iii) is safe.

Answer [   ]

Q28. (A2, 3) Global warming is good news for older people. Mortality rates are always higher in the winter than in the summer. Paradoxically, the wintertime 'excess mortality' in cold countries like Russia is lower than that of more moderate climates like the UK. People in cold countries are used to the cold and know more about keeping themselves warm than do people in temperate climates. However, the increasing prosperity of warmer countries helps to reduce winter deaths through reduced fuel poverty and people's ability to keep warm in their cars rather than having to rely on public transport.

Which two of the following can be concluded from the passage?

A. The increased prosperity of warmer countries mitigates the effects of winter on their excess mortality rates.
B. Global warming will reduce the winter excess mortality in Russia more than in the UK.
C. The paradox is that the outdoor temperature is not the only factor affecting winter mortality rates.
D. Both global warming and increasing prosperity will reduce excess mortality rates in the UK and Russia.
E. The ratio of deaths in winter to deaths in summer is lower in Russia than in the UK.

Answer [   ]

Q29. (A2, 3) Calculators should be banned from school until after pupils have mastered mental arithmetic. It is essential that young people can solve arithmetic problems in their heads or on paper without having to resort to a calculator. In medical sciences, over-reliance on calculators has led to fatal 'order of magnitude' errors because practitioners lacked the mental agility to estimate the answer to a drug dosage calculation or identify a wrong answer.

Which one of the following, if true, would lend the greatest support to the above argument?

A. Drug dosage calculation errors reflect a lack of calculator proficiency rather than a lack of mental arithmetic skills.
B. Practitioners who pass a mental arithmetic test make fewer drug dosage errors than those who fail the test.
C. Over-reliance on calculators leads to over-confidence in drug dosage calculations.
D. Practitioners who use calculators are less likely to identify drug dosages that are 10 times greater than they should be.

Answer [ ]

Q30. (M13c) The graph below shows the approximate incidence of prostate cancer and colorectal cancer in men per million men, between 1980 and 1994.

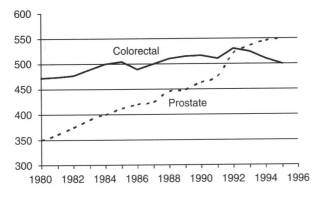

Reading from the graph, what was the average annual rate of increase in the incident rate of prostate cancer between 1984 and 1994 per million men?

A. 10
B. 13
C. 15
D. 18
E. 20

Answer [ ]

Q31. (M13c) If 10000 men were diagnosed with colorectal cancer in 1995, how many men were in the population group?

A. 10 million.
B. 20 million.
C. 25 million.
D. 30 million.
E. 1 million.

Answer ☐

Q32. Carl is younger than Zak but older than Richard. Leanne is older than Carl but younger than Sarah. Which of the following statements cannot be true?

A. Richard is the youngest.
B. Zak is the oldest.
C. Sarah is the same age as Zak.
D. Carl is the second oldest.
E. Leanne is younger than Zak.

(hint: draw a young-to-old continuum line)

Answer ☐

Q33. (M12b) A medical student sat two progress tests, T1 and T2. Each test was split into two sections, A and B, which were marked separately, and in the case of test T2 carried different weightings, as shown in the table. Calculate the combined percentage for the two tests (T1 and T2) if the marks for test T1 carry twice the weight of the marks for test T2.

	Test %		Weighting	
	A	B	A	B
Test T1	60%	72%	50%	50%
Test T2	90%	55%	40%	60%

(hint: per cent mark × decimal weight; add; 2/3, 1/3)

Answer ☐

Questions 34 and 35 refer to the following information:

'Passing off' is a term used when a business attempts to mislead customers into believing that they are dealing with a well-known, more established business, through the use of confusingly similar trade marks or trade names. For example, McDonald's has taken legal action against several businesses that refused to drop Mc from their trading name, including those with phonetically similar names such Macdonalds, Mcdonald. and Mcdonalds. The protection of a trading name is essential because associations with a lesser business can damage the reputation of an established business.

McDonald's has not always won its legal cases. However, it was more likely to succeed if the business had a clear association with a food service that could be confused with McDonald's. Thus, Elizabeth McCaughey was forced to change the name of her coffee shop from McCoffee and a Scottish sandwich shop owner had to change the name McMunchies, but McChina Wok Away was permitted because it was ruled that McChina would not cause any confusion amongst customers. It was also indicated that McDonald's did not have the right to the prefix Mc. Despite this ruling, McDonald's won its case against McCurry when a high court judge ruled that the use of the prefix Mc combined with colours distinctive of the McDonald's brand might confuse and deceive customers; the business had claimed that McCurry stood for Malaysian Chicken Curry.

Norman McDonald ran a small restaurant named McDonald's Hamburgers; Country drive-in. He fell foul of the McDonald's restaurant chain by including a couple of lit golden arches in his sign, making a play on the real McDonald's. He was forced to remove the arches and add Norman in front of McDonald's on the sign so as not to appear affiliated with the chain.

Q34. In which one of the following circumstance, is McDonald's most likely to win a 'passing off' lawsuit?

A. A breach of copyright law in using the term Mc.
B. Having the surname McDonald's as part of a sign's name.
C. Using McDonald's established reputation to benefit trade.
D. Any type of business placing Mc in front of its name.

Answer [   ]

Q35. In 2004, McDonald's filed a lawsuit against the fast-food restaurant McJoy in the Philippines. Which of the following was the most likely outcome of the court's decision?

A. McJoy changed its name to MyJoy.
B. McJoy retained its name.
C. McJoy was fined for defamation of the McDonald's name.
D. McDonald's lost the case and had to pay the court costs.

Answer [ ]

Section 2 Scientific knowledge and applications

Mock test 2

27 questions
Time allowed 30 minutes
No calculators

In this mock test, all of the questions come with their revision topics shown in paren-theses. For example, (P3b; M6d) means revise Physics topic 3b and Maths topic 6d; (B1a; C10b,c) means revise Biology topic 1a and Chemistry topics 10b and 10c. Some questions include a hint indicating the method of solution.

Q1.   (C1, 2) What is the combined total of protons, neutrons and electrons in Cu^{2+} cations?

A. 91
B. 93
C. 95
D. 97

Answer

Q2.   (P6d or P8d) A golf ball is hit from a tee. The vertical component of its velocity is 30 metres per second (m s^{-1}). Calculate the maximum height that it will reach, ignoring the influence of spin and air resistance. (1 kg = 10 N.)

(hint: energy)

Answer

Q3.   (B3) Look at the list (1 to 7) below and then choose the correct path for blood flowing through the heart to the lungs.
1. right ventricle; 2. bicuspid valve (mitral); 3. right atrium; 4. pulmonary artery; 5. pulmonary vein; 6. left atrium; 7. tricuspid valve.

A. 1, 2, 3, 4
B. 6, 2, 1, 5
C. 3, 2, 1, 5
D. 3, 7, 1, 4
E   3, 2, 1, 4

(hint: 'tricycle before bicycle')

Answer [   ]

Q4.   (C4b) 95 RON unleaded petrol contains 95 per cent octane, which combusts to produce carbon dioxide and water according to the following equation:

$$2C_8H_{18} + aO_2 = bCO_2 + cH_2O.$$

How many moles of water are produced from one mole of octane?

(hint: b first)

Answer [   ]

Q5.   (P12a,c) The head pivots on the atlas vertebra ('C1') at the top of the spine. The weight of the head acts 4 cm in front of the pivot and the neck muscles act 6 cm behind the pivot to support the weight. What is the force in newtons, to the nearest newton, exerted by the neck muscles to support a head weighing 4 kg? (Take g = 10 m s^{-2}.)

A. 6 N
B. 36 N
C. 60 N
D. 40 N
E   27 N

(hint: balance)

Answer [   ]

Q6. (P4a) A motorist travels from Birmingham to Blackpool, a distance of 120 miles, at an average speed of 60 miles per hour and then leaves Blackpool and returns to Birmingham at an average speed of 40 miles per hour. What was the average speed for the round trip?

A. 45 mph.
B. 48 mph.
C. 50 mph.
D. 54 mph.
E 58 mph.

(hint: time)

Answer ☐

Q7. (C3a) Which one of the following elements will not form an ionic compound with fluorine?

A. Potassium.
B. Aluminium.
C. Carbon.
D. Caesium.

Answer ☐

Q8. (P17d) What is the approximate cost of boiling 1.75 litres of water in a kettle that draws 13 amps at 230 volts for four minutes, if electricity costs 15 pence per kilowatt-hour?

A. 1 p
B. 0.5 p
C. 2 p
D. 3 p
E 4 p

(hint: volume irrelevant)

Answer ☐

Q9. (B2) Which of the following sequences described one half of a complete cycle of breathing?

A. Chest muscles contract, chest expands, chest pressure rises, air is expired.
B. Chest muscles contract, chest contracts, chest pressure rises, air is expired.
C. Chest muscles contract, chest expands, chest pressure falls, air is inspired.
D. Chest muscles relax, chest contracts, chest pressure falls, air is expired.
E   Chest muscles relax, chest expands, chest pressure falls, air is inspired.

Answer ☐

Q10. (C1, 2) Choose the correct word or term (labelled A to K) from the list below to match each numbered space (i to vi) in the following text. Some words or terms may be used more than once or not at all.

A = element; B = mixture; C = molecules; D = ions; E = proton; F = atoms; G = charge; H = reduced; I = solution; J = compound; K = oxidized.

Sulphuric acid, H_2SO_4, is a [...i...] of hydrogen, oxygen and sulphur [...ii...]. It is manufactured by burning the [...iii...] sulphur in air to form [...iv...] of sulphur dioxide. These are then [...v...] to sulphur trioxide, which is absorbed in sulphuric acid to form oleum. Sulphuric acid dissociates (ionizes) fully in water, making it a powerful [...vi...] donor and an oxidizing agent.

i = ...
ii = ...
iii = ...
iv = ...
v = ...
vi = ...

Q11. (P13e,f) Mains water flows through a series of pipes and taps as shown below:

Choose the correct answer from the choices given.

A. The water pressures at taps A, B and C are all equal.
B. The water pressure at tap A is greater than at tap B.
C. The water pressures at taps A and B are equal.
D. The water pressure at tap A is less than at tap C.

(hint: incompressible; inverse law)

Answer [   ]

Q12. (M2c, M10) If $x = (y+1)^{0.25} + 0.5$, calculate the value of y when $x = 2.5$.

Answer [   ]

Q13. (B6) A schematic diagram of a nephron is shown below. Where is the concentration of salt the highest?

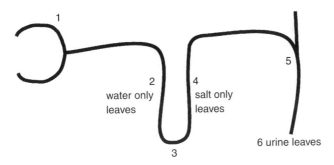

A. 1
B. 2
C. 3
D. 4
E   5

Answer [   ]

Q14. (C6b) Which two of the following gases dissolve in water and turn litmus paper red?

$A \ O_2$; $B \ CO$; $C \ CO_2$; $D \ HF$; $E \ NH_3$; $F \ CH_4$.

Answer

Q15. (P18c,d, 17d) What is the total equivalent resistance for the resistors arranged below?

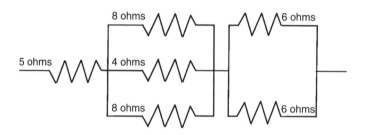

(hint: triple + pair + single)

Answer

Q16. (B8) According to the pedigree chart shown below, what is the probability of male M passing on an affected gene if he marries and has children, assuming that his wife is neither affected nor a carrier?

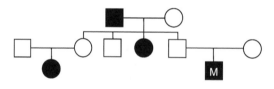

A. 100%.
B. 50%.
C. 33.3%.
D. 25%.
E. 0%.

Answer

Q17. (C5ii.iv) In a vehicle catalytic exhaust system the following pollutants are converted to less harmful emissions as follows:

i)   Carbon monoxide to carbon dioxide.
ii)   Hydrocarbons to carbon dioxide and water.
iii) Nitrogen oxides to nitrogen and oxygen.

Select the correct option (A to F) from the table below to describe the chemical reactions taking place in i), ii) and iii).

	Chemical reaction		
	i	ii	iii
A	oxidation	reduction	reduction
B	oxidation	de-hydration	reduction
C	reduction	oxidation	reduction
D	oxidation	oxidation	reduction
E	oxidation	reduction	oxidation

Answer ☐

Q18. (P7b) The three-car train shown below accelerates at 0.4 m s⁻². What is the tension in each of the three couplings?

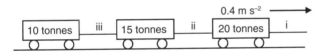

A. i) 8 kN ii) 6 kN iii) 4 kN
B. i) 18 kN ii) 18 kN iii) 18 kN
C. i) 18 kN ii) 12 kN iii) 8 kN
D. i) 18 kN ii) 10 kN iii) 4 kN

(hint: independently for each coupling)

Answer ☐

Q19. (M10, 11) A wallet contains £400 in £5, £10 and £20 notes. The number of £10 notes is twice the number of £5 notes and there are six fewer £20 notes than £10 notes. How many £5 notes are there?

Answer ☐

Q20. (C10b,c) Which *two* of the following statements are true about propene?

A. It is an alkane.
B. It burns in air to produce carbon monoxide and hydrogen.
C. It is an unsaturated hydrocarbon.
D. It has carbon–carbon triple bonds.
E. It turns bromine water colourless.

Answer ☐

Q21. (B2) The oxygen dissociation curve shows the percent saturation of haemoglobin versus the oxygen partial pressure. Which *two* of the following statements are true if the curve shifts to the right (dotted line) when a person begins to exercise?

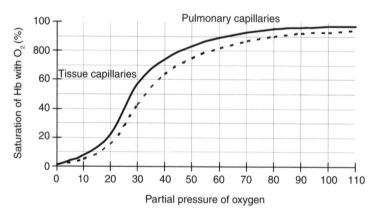

A. There is an increase in the oxygen saturation of haemoglobin at the lungs.
B. There is a decrease in the oxygen saturation of haemoglobin at the tissues.
C. There is an increase in the partial pressure of oxygen at the tissues.
D. There is a decrease in the oxygen saturation of haemoglobin at the lungs.
E. There is a decrease in the partial pressure of oxygen at the tissues.

(hint: for tissues compare 50% Hb saturation values; for lungs compare $P_{50\%}$ values)

Answer ☐

Q22. (M18b) Which of the following values of x satisfy the inequality $x(x-3) \leq 10$?

    A. $-3, -2, -1, 1, 0, 1, 2$
    B. $1, 2, 3, 4, 5, 6, 7$
    C. $-4, -3, -2, -1, 0, 1$
    D. $-1, 0, 1, 2, 3, 4, 5$
    E. $5, 6, 7, 8, 9, 10$

Answer ☐

Q23. (C9) The apparatus below shows the electrolysis of sodium chloride solution using carbon (inert) electrodes. Choose the correct substance or equation (labelled A to F) from the list below to match each label on the diagram (i to iv).

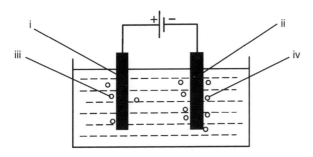

A: $2OH^- = O_2 + 2H_2O + 4e^-$
B: $2H_2O + 4e^- = 4OH^- + H_2$
C: $2Cl^- = Cl_2 + 2e^-$
D: Na
E: Cl_2
F: H_2

i = ...
ii = ...
iii = ...
iv = ...

Q24. (B7) How many strands of DNA are there in the chromosome shown below?

    A. 0
    B. 1
    C. 2
    D. 4
    E. 8

Answer ☐

Q25. (P16b) The energy of x-ray photons is given by $E = Fh$ where f is the frequency of the photons in hertz (Hz), h is Planck's constant (6.63×10^{-34}). If an x-ray photon has 1.2×10^{-15} joules of energy, how many photons are produced every second?

    A. 1.8×10^{18}
    B. 5.5×10^{48}
    C. 4.0×10^{34}
    D. 8.3×10^{20}
    E. 2.5×10^{18}

(hint: Hz = s^{-1})

Answer ☐

Q26. (M3, 4) Calculate $\dfrac{25 + \dfrac{1}{8}}{7 - \dfrac{3}{10}}$.

Answer ☐

Q27. (C9b, P15) The specific heat capacity of a substance is the energy required to raise 1 g by 1 °C; for water it is 4.2 J g^{-1} °C^{-1}. The heat of vaporization of a substance is the energy required to convert 1 g of liquid at its boiling point to gas at the same temperature; for water it is 2.3 kJ g^{-1}. Calculate the amount of energy required to raise 1 kg of water at 0 °C to boiling point and convert 200 g of it to steam. Give your answer in kilojoules.

Answer [   ]

Section 3 Writing task

Mock test 3

Choose one question
Time allowed 30 minutes; you have one side of A4 paper.
No dictionaries

1. Modern medicine has far more to do with science than with art

What do you understand by the above statement? Develop a unified argument that contradicts this opinion. Can you reconcile medicine as both art and science?

2. A little knowledge is a dangerous thing (Alexander Pope)

What is the author implying by this statement? Can a lot of knowledge be a more dangerous thing? Write a unified essay that argues the value in having a little knowledge.

3. Few people are capable of expressing with equanimity opinions that differ from the prejudices of their social environment. Most people are even incapable of forming such opinions (Albert Einstein)

What does the author mean by these comments and how would you refute them? Write a unified essay that includes examples of prejudices and how changes in attitudes and beliefs can be brought about.

Section 1 Aptitude and skills

Mock test 4

35 questions
Time allowed one hour
No calculators

Q1. (A2, 3) Studies on longevity have found that children born to mothers aged 25 and below are likely to live the longest. Longevity is further increased if the child is the firstborn. Younger mums bear offspring that are healthier, thrive better and are less prone to infections.

Which one of the following might be inferred from the above paragraph?

A. The ova of younger women are likely to be healthier than the ova of older women.
B. Longevity is inversely proportional to the age of the mother.
C. Mothers aged 25 and below are healthier than older mothers.
D. Younger mothers bear a higher proportion of females than older mothers and females live longer.

Answer ☐

Q2. (A2, 3) We should all buy locally farmed produce to reduce carbon emissions. Flying food halfway around the world might benefit poor farmers in developing countries but it increases its carbon footprint.

Which of the following is an implicit assumption of the above argument?

A. Food from poor farmers is flown halfway around the world.
B. Locally produced food has the lower carbon footprint.
C. Poor farmers are not as important as carbon emissions.
D. Local farmers are more important that poor farmers.
E. Buying local produce supports local farmers.

Answer ☐

Q3.   (A2, 3) The answer to road congestion is not to build more roads. Road building has continued apace over the last 10 years but so has congestion because the new roads have encouraged drivers to travel longer distances and make more journeys.

Which one of the following, if true, would seriously weaken the above argument?

A.   The money spent on public transport has declined over the last decade.
B.   When more roads are built the traffic soon fills to the new capacity.
C.   There are 5 million more vehicles on the road than there were a decade ago.
D.   Economic activity has increased over the last 10 years.

Answer ☐

Q4.   (P5) The graph shows the motion of a car over seven time intervals H, I, J, K, L and M.

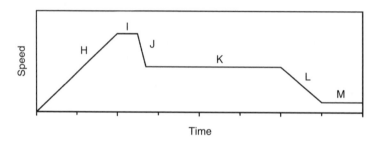

Which two intervals correspond with the greatest acceleration and the least displacement (distance)?

A.   H and I.
B.   H and K.
C.   J and I.
D.   J and M.
E.   H and M.

(hint: slopes and areas)

Answer ☐

Q5.   (M7b) A microwave oven is on sale with a 20 per cent discount. The following month the price is reduced by a further 10 per cent. What is the overall price reduction in percentage terms?

Answer [   ]

Q6.   (A2, 3) More than 50 per cent of the prison population re-offend once they are released. Building more prisons and handing down longer sentences will significantly reduce crime.

Statement: 10 per cent of crimes reach court.

Which of the following best describes how the short statement relates to the argument?

A.   It lends significant support to the argument.
B.   It restates the conclusion of the argument.
C.   It restates one of the premises of the argument.
D.   It neither supports nor challenges the argument.
E.   It presents a significant challenge to the argument.

Answer [   ]

Q7.   (A2, 3) The misuse of antibiotics has led to the spread of superbugs like MRSA. Doctors should know that most ear, nose and throat infections are self-limiting, which means that 90 per cent of prescriptions are unnecessary. The rise of superbugs is due to the over-eagerness of doctors to prescribe antibiotics.

Which one of the following shows that the conclusion is unsafe even if the evidence is correct?

A.   Patients with an infection expect their doctor to prescribe them antibiotics.
B.   In healthy people most MRSA infections are self-limiting.
C.   Doctors are only happy about writing prescriptions for the 10 per cent of patients who really need them.
D.   Superbugs would not have proliferated if antibiotics had not been over-prescribed.
E.   90 per cent of infections would have cleared up without the use of antibiotics.

Answer [   ]

Q8. Which one of the following letters will not look correct if it is turned upside down and reflected in a mirror?

B C I E X S

Answer [ ]

Q9. (M2e,iii) What is the missing letter in the table below?

?	B	D	C
C	A	B	F
B	E	C	B
D	D	C	A

Answer [ ]

Q10. (M13a,b) Which pie chart might display the same data as the bar chart?

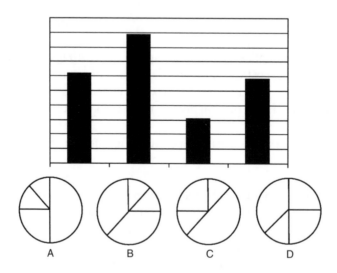

Answer [ ]

Q11. (M13c) The line graph shows the trend in the number of households with regular use of a car from 1960 to 2000. The graph shows that the number of one-car-only households has been stable at 45 per cent from about 1970.

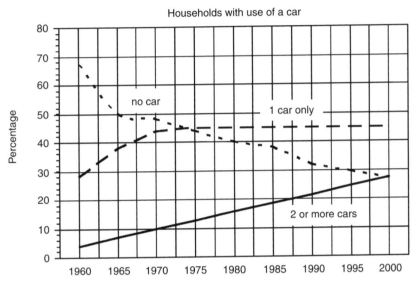

Households with use of a car

If trends continue, approximately when will the number of two or more car households equal the number of one-car households?

A. 2010
B. 2012
C. 2015
D. 2020
E. 2030

(hint: gradient)

Answer ☐

Q12. (M7b) By what fraction did no-car ownership decline between 1965 and 1995?

A. 1/5
B. 2/5
C. 1/2
D. 3/5
E. 4/5

Answer ☐

Q13. (M7b) If in the future, half of all households have the use of two or more cars, what percentage increase will this be compared with the 1970 figure?

A. 40%.
B. 400%.
C. 450%.
D. 500%.
E. 550%.

Answer [   ]

Q14. (A2, 3) Common sense dictates that in the event of an accident, the driver of a smaller car is more likely to be injured than the driver of a large car. Therefore, it is preferable to drive a big, polluting car and ignore the damage to the environment than to drive a small, environmentally friendly car and put your own safety at risk.

Which of the following is an unwarranted assumption of the above argument?

A. Car safety in an accident is a matter of common sense.
B. Bigger cars usually burn more fuel than smaller cars.
C. Personal safety is more important than damaging the environment.
D. You should never put your own safety at risk.
E. Occupants of smaller cars are more likely to be injured in an accident than occupants of larger cars.

Answer [   ]

Q15. (A2, 3) Discipline in schools has deteriorated since the abolishment of corporal punishment. School detention has not proved as effective as 'the cane' in deterring unruly behaviour. Disruptive pupils have a negative effect on the performance of a school because they reduce pupils' exposure to classroom instruction.

Which of the following can safely be inferred from the above paragraph?

A. Rewarding desirable behaviour in the classroom will improve school performance.
B. Poor performance in schools is linked with a lack of classroom discipline.
C. Bringing back 'the cane' is the best way to improve pupil behaviour.
D. Unruly behaviour is linked with anxiety over classroom performance.

Answer [   ]

Q16. (A2, 3) There is a clear link between MMR vaccinations and autism in children. The number of children diagnosed with autism has increased in proportion to the number of children receiving the triple vaccine. It can be concluded that an MMR vaccination increases the risk of a child developing autism.

Which of the following, if true, would show that the conclusion is unsafe even if the evidence is correct?

A. It can be difficult to diagnose autism differentially from Asperger's syndrome.

B. The number of cases of autism prior to the introduction of the MMR vaccine is unknown.

C. The age when MMR is given coincides with the age when autism is first diagnosed.

D. Many of the children diagnosed with autism have not had the MMR vaccine.

Answer [   ]

Q17. (A2, 3) Poverty in the UK can be defined in three ways: absolute, relative and social exclusion. People in absolute poverty are 'living below the breadline' with barely sufficient resources to sustain themselves. Relative poverty defines income and resources in relation to the national average (less than 60 per cent). Social exclusion is a new term that looks at the broader picture of unemployment, bad housing, crime levels, poor health and family breakdown as well as low incomes when attempting to define poverty.

Which of the following statements best summarizes the paragraph?

A. No person in the UK is in absolute poverty, 60 per cent are in relative poverty and less than 40 per cent are socially excluded.

B. Few people in the UK are in absolute poverty and those in relative poverty earn no more than 40 per cent of the national average wage.

C. There are more people in relative poverty in the UK than there are in absolute poverty and social exclusion together.

D. Poverty for the vast majority of people in the UK is a moral question concerned with the unequal distribution of resources in society.

E. Poverty cannot be defined in terms of low incomes without including social factors.

Answer [   ]

Q18. (A2, 3) Improvements in teaching and investment in schools have led to an increase in the number of medical and veterinary school applicants achieving triple-A grades. As a result, universities now have to rely on selection tests as a means of differentiating between the most able candidates.

Which two of the following if true would most seriously weaken the above argument?

A. Exam boards have maintained exam standards at the same level for the past ten years.
B. Students do not have to work as hard as in the past.
C. Candidates sitting selection tests are achieving higher marks every year.
D. Exam boards are making A-levels easier to pass.
E. The exam marks of first-year university students are getting worse every year.

Answer [   ]

Q19. (M14a,b, M19c,i) The box and whisker plot summarizes the performance of 500 students in the first two sections of the BMAT.

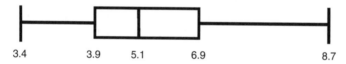

3.4   3.9   5.1   6.9   8.7

What is the probability that if two students are chosen at random one will have achieved four marks or more and one will have achieved seven marks or more?

A. 1/2
B. 1/4
C. 1/8
D. 1/16
E. 3/16

Answer [   ]

Q20. (A2, 3) Place the following four sentences in the order in which they form the most coherent passage.

A. The need for bipedal locomotion may have arisen when climate change forced apes to live more on the ground than in the trees.

B. Another theory is that the brain grew after humans stopped walking on all fours.

C. Some anthropologists have hypothesized that the human brain developed when people began using their hands as tools.

D. Walking upright preceded development of the hand, which was then free to develop, unhindered by walking.

Answer [   ]

Q21. (M13b) The stacked bar chart shows the number of pupils with special educational needs (SEN) and without SEN in five schools, V, W, X, Y and Z.

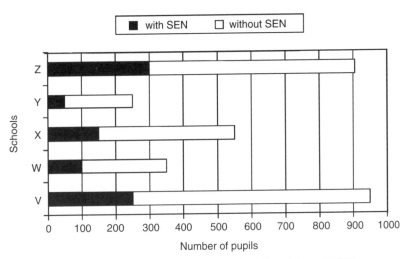

Which school had the lowest proportion of pupils without SEN?

A. Z
B. Y
C. X
D. W
E. V

Answer [   ]

Q22. (M13b) According to the stacked bar chart, what percent of the total pupils with SEN in all five schools are found among the *two* schools with the most pupils having SEN? Give your answer to the nearest whole percent.

A. 65%
B. 29%
C. 70%
D. 32%
E. 55%

Answer ☐

Q23. (M13b, M7) If 40% of the pupils with SEN are on free school meals and there are a total of 426 pupils on free school meals in all five schools, what per cent of the pupils without SEN are *not* on free school meals?

A. 45%.
B. 12%.
C. 4%.
D. 8%.
E. 50%.

Answer ☐

Q24. (A4a) Out of 18 candidates who sat a BMAT, 12 held an A level in Chemistry and 11 held an A level in Biology. Some candidates held both subjects and no candidate held neither subject. How many candidates held A-level Chemistry but not A-level Biology?

A. 4
B. 5
C. 6
D. 7
E. 8

(hint: two-circle problem; let n = the overlap)

Answer ☐

Q25. (M10a,b) What volume of 1.0 molar saline solution must be added to 500 ml of 6.0 molar saline solution to dilute it to a 2.0 molar solution? (1 molar = 1 mol/L)

A. 750 ml
B. 1.0 L
C. 1.5 L
D. 1.75 L
E. 2.0 L

(hint: algebra; add x litres; moles constant)

Answer ▢

Q26. (M13e) Anti-hypertensive drugs are an important method of controlling high blood pressure (BP). There are four main *classes* of drug, namely ACE inhibitors (A), beta-blocker (B), calcium channel blockers (C) and diuretics (D). Table 1 shows the preferred choice of drugs as well as those to avoid (contraindicated).

Table 2 shows which treatment options are preferred in patients with diabetes. ACE inhibitors (A) are the first choice of treatment and these can be combined with other classes of drugs to provide a sufficient reduction in blood pressure.

Table 1: Anti-hypertensive drugs: indications and contra-indications

	Indicated in:	Contraindicated in:
class A	heart failure, CHD	renovascular disease, pregnancy
class B	angina, MI	asthma, COPD, heart block
class C	angina	heart block, heart failure
class D	heart failure	gout

legend: CHD = coronary heart disease; MI = myocardial infarction; COPD = chronic obstructive pulmonary disease

Table 2: Treatment options for BP control in patients with diabetes

	Treatment options
Step 1	A
Step 2	A + C
Step 3	A + C + D
Step 4	A + C + D + F

D = thiazide diuretic;
F = furosemide diuretic

legend: CHD = coronary heart disease; MI = myocardial infarction; COPD = chronic obstructive pulmonary disease

According to Tables 1 and 2, what would be the next treatment option for a patient with diabetes and heart failure, whose blood pressure remains elevated despite ACE inhibitor therapy?

A. Beta-blocker.
B. Calcium channel blocker.
C. Thiazide diuretic.
D. Calcium channel blocker + diuretic.
E. Furosemide diuretic.

Answer [   ]

Q27. A patient with diabetes, angina and asthma remains hypertensive despite ACE inhibitor therapy. What would be the next treatment option to consider?

A. Beta-blocker.
B. Calcium channel blocker.
C. Thiazide diuretic.
D. Calcium channel blocker + diuretic.
E. Furosemide diuretic.

Answer [   ]

Q28. In a darts tournament two teams of 16 players each are drawn against each other and the winners go forward to the next round. Two players fail to turn up and their opponents are given an automatic win. What is the total number of matches that will have to be played to find a winner?

A. 32
B. 31
C. 30
D. 29
E. 28

Answer [   ]

Q29. (M10a) A round of toast and a portion of margarine cost £1.10. The toast costs £1 more than the margarine. How much does the round of toast cost?

A. £0.90
B. £0.95
C. £1.00
D. £1.05
E. £1.15

Answer [   ]

Q30. (M9a,e) A solid sphere fits neatly inside a hollow cube. The volume of the sphere is given by its radius cubed multiplied by four-thirds pi (π). What is the ratio of the volume of the sphere to the volume of the cube?

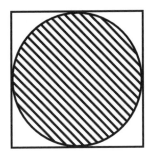

A. 6π
B. $32/3\pi$
C. $2/3\pi$
D. $6/\pi$
E. $\pi/6$

Answer [   ]

Q31. (A2, 3) Tax on cigarettes means that smokers' contributions to the economy far outweigh what they cost the NHS in treating smoking-related diseases. Therefore, the tax raised on smoking benefits the economy for both smokers and non-smokers alike.

Which of the following, if true, identifies the most significant flaw in the argument's conclusion?

A. Tax raised on cigarettes is not necessarily spent on the NHS.
B. The money smokers would save by not smoking would generate other tax revenues for the economy.
C. The social costs of smoking and the suffering it causes far outweigh the financial benefits.
D. The money spent on smokers is not limited to NHS treatment.

Answer ☐

Q32. (A2, 3) Patients cannot undergo medical treatment without first giving their informed consent, either implied, verbal or written. However, in a medical emergency when a patient is unconscious, consent to treatment may be presumed unless there has been a prior expression of a refusal to consent in that emergency situation.

If the paragraph is true, which of the following statements must be false?

A. Patients must know what they are consenting to and have the right to refuse medical interventions.
B. Consent is never presumed in a conscious patient but is normally presumed in an unconscious patient.
C. The patient's prior wish to refuse treatment is often ignored in situations where there is a risk to the patient's life.
D. Doctors are sometimes allowed to act in what they know to be the best interests of their patients.
E. Doctors must always act to save the patient's life unless the patient has explicitly forbidden it in writing.

Answer ☐

Q33. (P4a) Zak cycles to university at an average speed of 12 miles per hour and Phoebe walks the same route at an average speed of 3 miles per hour. If Phoebe sets out at 08.30 hrs and Zak sets out 15 minutes later, what time will it be when he catches her up?

    A. 08.45
    B. 08.50
    C. 08.55
    D. 09.00
    E. 09.05

(hint: same distance d; Phoebe: $d = st$; Zak $d = $?)

Question 34 and 35 refer to the following information:

People who abuse alcohol are motivated to reduce their consumption when the adverse consequences outweigh the perceived benefits. Disulfiram (Antabuse®) is an adjunct therapy that is used to help maintain abstinence in patients who abuse alcohol. People who consume even a small amount of alcohol after taking disulfiram medication experience symptoms similar to a 'hangover', including nausea and vomiting, which makes the drug a powerful alcohol deterrent; a 12-hour period of abstinence is necessary before commencing disulfiram therapy. Alcoholism is a disease characterized by dependency where the abuser is no longer able to control his/her intake and cannot stop drinking under any circumstances.

Research suggests that genetics and a family history of alcoholism predispose some people to dependency; other people remain free of dependency. Alcohol-induced liver disease can progress from steatosis (fatty liver), to alcoholic hepatitis and finally alcoholic cirrhosis. Steatosis is reversible when the drinking stops. Drinking heavily for longer periods may give rise to alcoholic hepatitis where fat becomes inflamed and the damage takes several weeks to resolve after the patient stops drinking. In alcoholic cirrhosis the damaged cells are replaced by permanent scar tissue and if the drinking continues, the consequences can be fatal.

Patients with alcoholic liver disease may present with jaundice, hepatic encephalopathy (damage to the brain and nervous system) and ascites (fluid in the abdomen), which is caused by portal vein hypertension. The blood pressure increases in the portal vein because the blood cannot flow normally from the digestive organs to the liver. Portal vein hypertension may lead to oesophageal varices (dilated veins), and if these rupture, the mortality rate is very high.

Q34. Which two of the following statements can be inferred from the passage?

    A. Disulfiram is not the primary treatment for alcohol abuse.
    B. Disulfiram is unsuitable for patients who are dependent on alcohol.
    C. Alcoholism can run in families though there is no genetic trait.
    D. Any alcohol-induced liver disease is reversible if the patient stops in time.

Answer [   ]

Q35. Which two of the following statements can be inferred from the passage?

    A. Chronic alcohol abuse eventually leads to dependency.
    B. Chronic alcohol abuse may lead to brain damage.
    C. Alcohol abuse is a disease process.
    D. The hepatic portal vein drains blood from the liver.
    E. A swollen abdomen and a jaundiced appearance are consistent with alcohol abuse or alcohol dependency.

Answer [   ]

Section 2 Scientific knowledge and applications

Mock test 5

27 questions
Time allowed 30 minutes
No calculators

Q1.   (C4a) Calcium hydrogen carbonate $Ca(HCO_3)_2$ is a buffer in the body. How many moles of oxygen are present in 0.5 mole of $Ca(HCO_3)_2$?

    A. 0.5
    B. 2.0
    C. 1.5
    D. 6.0
    E. 3.0

(hint: atoms)

Answer [   ]

Q2.   (P20b) A radioisotope is being used for a medical procedure. The table shows how the sample decays with time. What was the activity of the sample when it was prepared?

Time: days	Activity: counts per minute
0	
1	3.2×10^5
2	8×10^4
3	2×10^4
4	5000

    A. 6.4×10^4
    B. 1.28×10^6
    C. 2.56×10^6
    D. 5.12×10^5

(hint: half-life)

Answer [   ]

Q3.   (B3) Identify the correct path for blood flowing through the heart to the body.

    A.   Left atrium, tricuspid valve, left ventricle, aorta.
    B.   Left atrium, bicuspid (mitral) valve, left ventricle, pulmonary artery.
    C.   Left atrium, bicuspid (mitral) valve, left ventricle, aorta.
    D.   Right atrium, pulmonary valve, right ventricle, pulmonary artery.
    E.   Right atrium, tricuspid valve, right ventricle, pulmonary artery.

Answer [ ]

Q4.   (C5ii) In which of the following compounds does oxygen have the highest oxidation number?

    A. H_2O
    B. O_2
    C. H_2O_2
    D. CO_2
    E. OF_2

(hint: 0, –,+)

Answer [ ]

Q5.   (P10a,7e) A golf ball of mass 46 g is hit from a tee peg at a speed of 50 m s^{-1}. If the ball is in contact with the golf club for 10 milliseconds, what force is exerted on the club face?

(hint: change in momentum)

Answer [ ]

Q6.   (M9a) If the area of the square is 9 cm^2, what is the area of the circle?

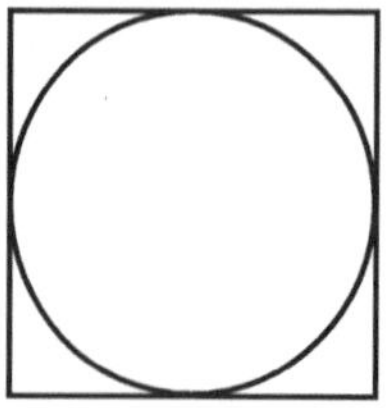

    A. 2π
    B. 2.25π
    C. 2.5π
    D. 3π
    E. 3.25π

Answer [ ]

Q7.   (C1, 2) Which of the following statements could be true for the element krypton?

A.   36 protons, 36 neutrons, 36 electrons, 6 isotopes.
B.   83.8 protons and neutrons and 36 electrons.
C.   36 protons and 36 electrons, 6 isotopes.
D.   6 isotopes, 36 protons, 36 electrons, 84 neutrons.

Answer [   ]

Q8.   (P18d) In the diagram, what current flows through the bulb?

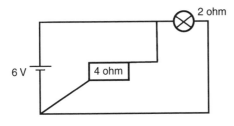

A.   1 A
B.   4 A
C.   3 A
D.   8 A
E.   6 A

(hint: parallel; bulb)

Answer [   ]

Q9. (B5) Choose the correct word or term (labelled A to K) from the list below to match each numbered space (i to ix) in the following text. Some words may be used more than once or not at all.

A = pituitary; B = less; C = metabolism; D = more; E = hypothalamus; F = hot; G = endocrine; H = hormones; I = cold; J = thyroid; K = exocrine

The [...i...] is the gland of the [...ii...] system responsible for [...iii...]. It secretes the [...iv...] T3 and T4 into the bloodstream in response to thyroid-stimulating hormone (TSH) released by the [...v...] gland. This latter gland is adjacent to and regulated by the [...vi...] region of the brain. Thus in [...vii...] weather the brain signals the [...viii...] gland to release [...ix...] TSH.

i = ...
ii = ...
ii = ...
iv = ...
v = ...
vi = ...
vii = ...
viii = ...
ix = ...

Q10. (C10b) Bromine water can be used to distinguish between alkanes and alkenes because bromine reacts with alkenes by adding to both sides of the double bond. Which two of the following hydrocarbons will turn bromine water colourless?

A. C_2H_6
B. C_3H_6
C. $C_{12}H_{26}$
D. $C_{20}H_{42}$
E. $C_{60}H_{120}$

(hint: draw/general formula?)

Answer ☐

Q11. (P8a,b) Ali (A), Ben (B), Chris (C) and Dave (D) lift weights at the gym.
Ali can lift 25 kg 12 times in 20 seconds.
Ben can lift 35 kg 10 times in 35 seconds.
Chris can lift 40 kg 5 times in 20 seconds.
Dave can lift 60 kg once in 5 seconds.

Choose the correct answer A, B, C or D if all the weights are lifted through a distance of 1 metre.

(hint: work done)

A. Dave uses the least energy but develops the most power.
B. Ben uses the most energy and develops the most power.
C. Ali develops the most power but does not use the most energy.
D. Chris uses more energy than Dave and develops more power than him.

Answer [   ]

Q12. (M6) What is $5.2 \times 10^{12} + 4.8 \times 10^{11} - 1.0 \times 10^{10}$ in scientific notation?

A. 5.68×10^{12}
B. 5.67×10^{12}
C. 5.67×10^{11}
D. 56.7×10^{10}
E. 5.60×10^{12}

Answer [   ]

Q13. (P13a, 3e) Lead ingots measuring 200 mm × 100 mm × 50 mm are stacked with their largest face on the ground. (1 kg = 10 N.)

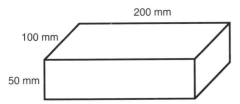

200 mm

100 mm

50 mm

If the density of lead is approximately 11 gram per cm³, what pressure in pascals (Pa) will an ingot exert on the ground?

(hint: 1 Pa = 1 N m⁻²)

Answer [   ]

Q14. (B6) A schematic diagram of a nephron is shown below. Identify the correct transport processes from 1 through to 5.

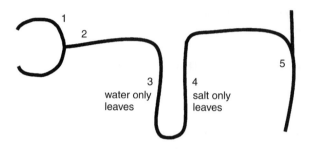

3
water only
leaves

4
salt only
leaves

A. Ultrafiltration, active transport, osmosis, active transport, osmosis.
B. Diffusion, active transport, osmosis, active transport, osmosis.
C. Ultrafiltration, re-absorption, countercurrent, active transport, excretion.
D. Ultrafiltration, osmosis, active transport, osmosis, diffusion.
E. Ultrafiltration, re-absorption, diffusion, active transport, active transport.

Answer ☐

Q15. (C7iii) The pH of blood is maintained at 7.4 by the carbonic acid hydrogen carbonate ion buffer as follows:

$$CO_2 + H_2O = H^+ + HCO_3^-.$$

Which of the following statements is consistent with respiratory acidosis of the blood?

A. CO_2 levels rise and the pH falls.
B. CO_2 levels rise and the pH remains unchanged.
C. CO_2 levels rise and the pH rises.
D. CO_2 levels fall and the pH rises.

Answer ☐

Q16. (C9iii) The apparatus below shows the electrolysis of a strong solution of hydro-chloric acid using carbon (inert) electrodes. Choose the correct substance or equation (labelled A to G) from the list below to match each label on the diagram (i to iv):

A: $2OH^- \rightarrow O_2 + 2H_2O + 4e^-$
B: $2H^+ + 2e^- \rightarrow H_2$
C: $2Cl^- \rightarrow Cl_2 + 2e^-$
D: Na
E: Cl_2
F: H_2
G: O_2

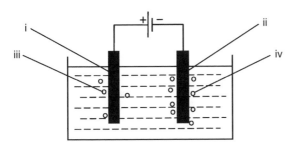

i = ...
ii = ...
iii = ...
iv = ...

Q17. (B8) What type of inheritance is shown in the diagram below if F is not a carrier for the disease?

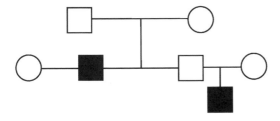

key: male = ☐ female = ◯ affected/disease = shaded

   A. Autosomal dominant.
   B. Autosomal recessive.
   C. X-linked dominant.
   D. X-linked recessive.
   E. Autosomal recessive or X-linked recessive.

Answer ☐

Q18. (P7a,b,e) A rightward force is applied to a 12-kg object to move it across a rough surface at constant velocity. The object encounters 30 N of frictional force.

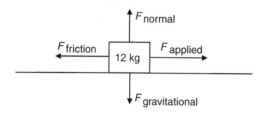

$(g = 10 \text{ m s}^{-2})$

Use the diagram to determine to the following forces:

A. gravitational force = ...
B. normal force = ...
C. applied force = ...
D. net force = ...

(hint: Newton's three laws: acceleration?)

Q19. (M9a) What is the area of the shaded region if the diameter of the circle is x?

A. $x^2 - \pi x^2$
B. $x^2(1 - 4\pi)$
C. $x^2(1 - \pi)/4$
D. $x^2(4 - \pi)/4$
E. $x^2 \pi /4 - \pi$

Answer ⬚

Q20. (C10c) Choose the word or term (labelled A to I) from the list below to match each numbered space (i to v) in the following text. Some words or terms may be used more than once or not at all.

A = melting points; B = boiling points; C = densities; D = volatile;
E = hydrocarbon; F = inorganic; G = liquid; H = top; I = bottom.

Fractional distillation of crude oil relies on the difference in the [...i...] of the [...ii...] constituents. The more [...iii...] fractions have the lowest [...iv...] and go to the [...v...] of the tower.

i = ...
ii = ...
ii = ...
iv = ...
v = ...

Q21. (B4a,b) Which of the following sequences describes the path of a nerve impulse in a reflex arc?

A. Receptor, efferent neurone, PNS, motor neurone, effector.
B. Receptor, afferent neurone, PNS, motor neurone, effector.
C. Receptor, effector, CNS, afferent neurone, efferent neurone.
D. Receptor, efferent neurone, CNS, afferent neurone, effector.
E. Receptor, afferent neurone, CNS, efferent neurone, effector.

(hint: 'effluent' away (from brain))

Answer [   ]

Q22. (P7b,d) In a hammer-throwing contest a competitor whirls a mass of 4 kg around her body in a circle. If the speed of rotation of the hammer is one revolution per second before letting go, what is the size of the force acting on the competitor's arms? The acceleration (a) of a rotating mass (m) towards the centre of rotation is given by $a = v^2/r$ where r is the radius of the circle and v the tangential velocity.

A. $16\pi^2 r$ N
B. $8\pi^2 r$ N
C. $4\pi r$ N
D. πr N
E. $8\pi^2 r^2$ N

(hint: speed, distance, time)

Answer [ ]

Q23. (M19, 20) Five cards are picked in turn from a shuffled pack of 52 playing cards. The first four cards are the Jack of Spades, King of Hearts, Queen of Diamonds and Jack of Clubs. What is the probability that the next card will not be another face (court) card?

A. 1/6
B. 5/6
C. $12/52 \times 11/51 \times 10/50 \times 9/49$
D. 5/52
E. 1/13

Answer [ ]

Q24. (B8(1)) Choose the word or term (labelled A to I) from the list below to match each numbered space (i to vi) in the following text. Some words or terms may be used more than once or not at all.

A = gene; B = genotype; C = chromosome; D = homozygous; E = allele; F = heterozygous; G = phenotype; H = zygote.

In determining inheritance, a [...i...] is a section of a [...ii...] that codes for a particular protein or characteristic. Each [...iii...], dominant or recessive, determines the type of coding for a trait. If these are the same the [...iv...] will have a homozygous [...v...] but if they are different the dominant one will determine the [...vi...].

i = ...
ii = ...
ii = ...
iv = ...
v = ...
vi = ...

Q25. (C2) Nitric oxide reacts with oxygen to produce nitrogen dioxide according to the following equation:

$$2NO_{(g)} + O_{2(g)} = 2NO_{2(g)}$$

Which one of the following statements is false?

A. Nitric oxide is a mixture of nitrogen and oxygen.
B. Oxygen is an element and a diatomic molecule.
C. Nitrogen dioxide is a compound and a molecule.
D. The mass of reactants equals the mass of products.
E. Three moles of reactants produce two moles of products.

Answer [   ]

Q26. What is the length of the diagonal line drawn inside the cube of side x?

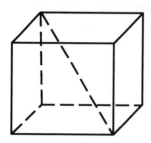

A. $2x$
B. $x\sqrt{2}$
C. $x\sqrt{3}$
D. $3\sqrt{2}x$
E. $(x/2)\sqrt{3}$

(hint: extra line; Pythag. two triangles)

Answer [ ]

Q27. (C9, P14a, P15) The graph shows the time–temperature curve of pure water when heated at atmospheric pressure.

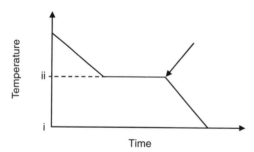

Which of the following statements are true and which are false?

A. There is one phase with two phase changes.
B. The temperature at i must be 273 K.
C. The temperature at ii must be 373 K.
D. Adding impurities to the water will increase ii.
E. The temperature at ii is lower on Mount Everest.

A. ......
B. ......
C. ......
D. ......
E. ......

Section 3 Writing task

Mock test 6

Choose one question
Time allowed 30 minutes; you have one side of A4 paper
No dictionaries

1. If we knew what we were doing, it would not be called research, would it? (Albert Einstein)

What do you think the author means by this? Can you advance a counter-argument? Are new facts derived from experimental research or are they derived from what is already known?

2. The female of the species is no longer the weaker sex

Explain what you believe the author means in making this statement. Discuss the claim in relation to men and women. Provide examples that support or refute the statement.

3. Medicine is a science of uncertainty and an art of probability (William Osler)

What does the author mean by this statement? How might his view relate to diagnosis and decision making?

Section 1 Aptitude and skills

Mock test 7

35 questions
Time allowed one hour
No calculators

Q1. (P5) The graph shows the motion of a power-boat over seven time intervals H, I, J, K, L and M.

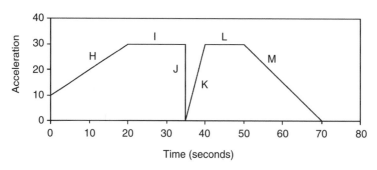

In which time interval is the change in velocity of the power-boat the greatest?

A. H
B. I
C. J
D. K
E. M

Answer ☐

Q2. (M7b) A jeweller buys a watch and marks the price up 80 per cent before selling it to a customer. What percentage of the customer's price is the jeweller's purchase cost? Give your answer to the nearest whole number.

Answer ☐

Q3. (A2, 3) Fractures of the hip are a leading cause of disability and mortality in elderly people. A high proportion of these patients have osteoporosis, which leads to fragile bones. All elderly people should take calcium and vitamin D supplements to help to prevent osteoporosis. This inexpensive treatment will reduce the risk of a hip fracture after a fall.

Which one of the following, if true, would seriously weaken the above argument?

A. Most falls in the elderly do not lead to bone fractures.
B. Preventive treatments are not cost-effective.
C. Most fractures involve vertebrae and not the hip.
D. Most elderly people do not have falls.
E. Regular exercise is the best way to strengthen bones.

Answer [   ]

Q4. (A2, 3) Placebo-controlled drug trials are unethical if participants are denied new therapeutic treatments that might prove effective. Any new treatment should be tested alongside the existing standard therapies to offer candidates the possibility of a better outcome and not just a 'nothing' treatment.

Which two of the following, if true, would most seriously weaken the above argument?

A. There is no guarantee that any new treatment will be any more effective than a placebo.
B. It is unethical to employ treatments that have not been proven safe or effective in a placebo-controlled drug trial.
C. In a placebo-based drug trial the participant loses the benefit of the standard treatment.
D. Placebo treatments are frequently effective and should not be described as 'nothing' treatments.

Answer [   ]

Q5.   (A2, 3) A five-year study has shown that obesity is caused by a sedentary lifestyle and not by over-eating. Participants with sedentary lifestyles put on more weight than participants who ate more.

Which of the following statements, if true, would make the findings of the study unsafe?

A.   Participants who put on more weight also dieted more.
B.   Participants who over-ate preferred fast food.
C.   Not all of the participants with a sedentary lifestyle put on weight.
D.   A sedentary lifestyle led to an increased food intake.
E.   A few participants lost weight during the five-year study.

Answer [ ]

Q6.   (M3a) If the shapes drawn below are placed inside the square frame, what fraction of the frame will be empty?

A.   1/16
B.   1/10
C.   1/8
D.   1/6
E.   1/4

Answer [ ]

Q7. Norton is west of Nettlestone, which is east of Niton. Ningwood is east of Norton and west of Niton. Newbridge is east of Niton, which is west of Norwood.

Norwood must be east of:

A. Norton, Ningwood and Niton.
B. Norton, Ningwood but not necessarily Niton.
C. Norton, Ningwood, Niton and Newbridge.
D. Ningwood, Niton and Newbridge only.
E. Norton, Ningwood and Niton but west of Newbridge.

(hint: horizontal line)

Answer ▢

Q8. (M20) A 50-year-old woman has an abnormal mammogram. Use the probability tree to calculate the chances she has of having breast cancer (CB). Give your answer as a percentage to one decimal place.

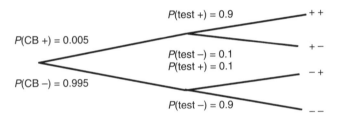

P(test +) = 0.9   + +

P(CB +) = 0.005

P(test −) = 0.1   + −
P(test +) = 0.1

P(CB −) = 0.995   − +

P(test −) = 0.9   − −

A. 4.3 per cent.
B. 4.4 per cent.
C. 4.5 per cent.
D. 4.8 per cent.
E. 5.0 per cent.

(hint: true positive + false positive; 1.0 = 100 per cent)

Answer ▢

Q9. (M13b) The bar chart shows the proportion of excess winter deaths by age and sex in England and Wales.

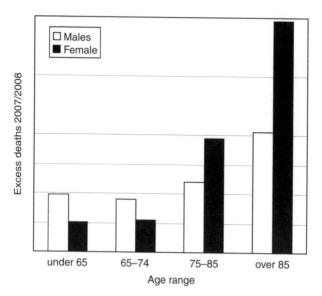

In percentage terms, approximately how many fewer male excess winter deaths were there than female excess winter deaths?

A. 26%.
B. 28%.
C. 32%.
D. 36%.
E. 40%.

Answer [ ]

Q10. (M13) Which of the columns in the table shows the correct number of excess winter deaths per 1000 of population consistent with the bar chart?

Age range	A	B	C	D	E
under 65	2	1	3	3	3
65–74	1.9	1.2	2.9	2.9	2.9
75–85	2.2	3.9	6.1	6.1	6.9
over 85	4.1	7.9	12	7.9	14

Answer [ ]

Q11. (M13) If there are approximately 25 000 excess deaths in total, how many of these were females aged 85 or over?

A. 6250
B. 8300
C. 10 000
D. 12 500
E. 15 000

Answer ⬚

Q12. (M7a) Estimate the population of England and Wales if the 25 000 excess deaths represent 0.048 per cent of the population.

A. 50 million.
B. 51 million.
C. 52 million.
D. 53 million.
E. 54 million.

Answer ⬚

Q13. (A2, 3) 'Grey power' is increasing at an alarming rate. More than a third of UK voters are now over age 55. Furthermore, the tendency for young people not to vote means that older people will constitute 50 per cent of the active voters by 2020. This might not matter if older voters acted in the best interests of society but they do not. Older people want increased pensions, better healthcare and free public transport for the elderly, and it is the young who are going to have to pay for it.

Which of the following best summarizes the argument?

A. Older people are motivated by self-interest and expect young people to pay for their needs.
B. The increasing proportion of older people in society has made them a powerful interest group.
C. An increasingly older electorate will act in their own interests to ensure more resources are allocated to them.
D. Taxes will have to rise if the needs of older people are going to be met.

Answer ⬚

Q14. (A2, 3) Studies suggest that the more violence and aggression teenagers watch on television, the more aggressive they are likely to be to the people around them. Violent computer games also promote violence and these should be banned altogether. The best way to reduce real-life violence is to restrict teenagers' access to images of violence on the screen.

Which of the following is the best statement of the flaw in the above argument?

A. It would be better to modify children's attitudes towards violence and aggression before restricting access to it.
B. Children have the same human rights as adults and can choose what they want to watch on television.
C. Several childhood factors are known to influence teenage aggression.
D. Parents have a responsibility to moderate the viewing habits of their children.
E. Only children with prior psychiatric disorders are likely to exhibit aggressive tendencies.

Answer [ ]

Q15. (A2, 3) There has been a 10 per cent decline in the number of people taking out a gym membership. As a nation we are becoming less interested in fitness.

Which of the following is an implicit assumption of the above argument?

A. Ten per cent of people leaving gyms are not interested in fitness.
B. Gym membership is the best way of maintaining fitness.
C. Unless you work out at a gym you will not keep fit.
D. Ninety per cent of people join gyms to keep fit.
E. Unless you join a gym you are not interested in fitness.

Answer [ ]

Q16. (A2, 3) Prostate-specific antigen (PSA) levels are raised in men with prostate cancer. A study suggests that PSA levels get diluted in obese men because of their greater blood volume. Consequently it can be too late to treat obese men who have prostate cancer detected by a PSA test.

Statement: The total amount of PSA in obese men with prostate cancer is higher than it is in men of average weight with prostate with cancer.

Which of the following best describes how the statement relates to the study?

A. It neither supports or challenges the argument.
B. It is inconsistent with the findings of the study.
C. It restates the conclusion of the argument.
D. It restates one of the premises of the argument.
E. It is consistent with the finding of the study.

Answer ☐

Q17. (M2c) In DNA fingerprinting, the probability of one band matching is given by $p = 0.5$, or 1 in 2. The probability of two bands matching is given by $p = (0.5)^2$ or 1 in 4. If the population of the UK is approximately 60 million, how many bands need to be compared to be confident that one match will not happen by chance?

A. 30 bands.
B. 26 bands.
C. 20 band.
D. 14 bands.
E. 10 bands.

(hint: $(1/2)^x = 1/2^x$)

Answer ☐

Q18. (M14b) The box and whisker plot summarizes the performance of 200 students in the first two sections of the BMAT.

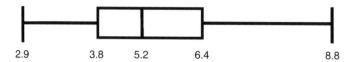

2.9　　　3.8　5.2　　　6.4　　　　　　8.8

Indicate all the false statements:

A.　At least one student achieved 8.8 marks on the BMAT scale.
B.　Half the students scored between 3.8 and 6.4 marks.
C.　One-quarter of the pupils scored more than 3.8 marks.
D.　The mean mark was 5.2.
E.　The probability that two students chosen at random achieved more than 6.4 marks is 6.25 per cent.

A. = ...
B. = ...
C. = ...
D. = ...
E. = ...

Q19. (M13a) A high-calorie drink is available to patients in neutral, vanilla and chocolate flavours. The pie chart shows the popularity of the three flavours amongst patients.

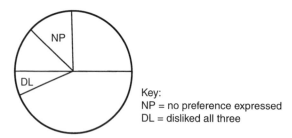

Key:
NP = no preference expressed
DL = disliked all three

Which one of the following columns might represent preferences expressed?

Flavour	A	B	C	D	E
neutral	30	90	160	500	160
vanilla	60	120	320	300	80
chocolate	120	400	320	200	280

Answer [   ]

Q20. (M13b) The stacked bar chart shows retailers' annual book sales in four categories: children's (CH), adult non-fiction (AN), adult special (AS) and adult fiction (AF).

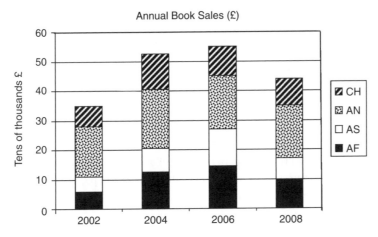

In which year did the smallest proportion of sales come from children's books?

A. 2002
B. 2004
C. 2006
D. 2008

Answer ☐

Q21. (M7b) Approximately what is the increase in per cent in annual sales between the years with the greatest difference?

A. 20 per cent.
B. 40 per cent.
C. 49 per cent.
D. 57 per cent.
E. 66 per cent.

Answer ☐

Q22. (M13b) According to the stacked bar chart, approximately what was the greatest increase in adult fiction sales over any two-year span?

A. £10000
B. £60000
C. £120000
D. £150000
E. £175000

Answer ☐

Q23. John has 36 books that are either paperbacks or hardbacks. One-quarter are fiction books and 24 are paperbacks. There are six times as many paperback non-fiction books as hardback fiction books. How many books does he have that are both hardback and non-fiction?

A. 2
B. 4
C. 6
D. 8
E. 9

(hint: 2 × 2 table; tally rows and columns)

Answer ☐

Q24. (P3c) Water drips from a tap at a rate of one drop every three seconds. The volume of water in each drop is 0.1 ml. If the tap is left to drip for 25 hours, how many litres of water will be wasted?

Answer ☐

Q25. Which shape does not belong with the other four?

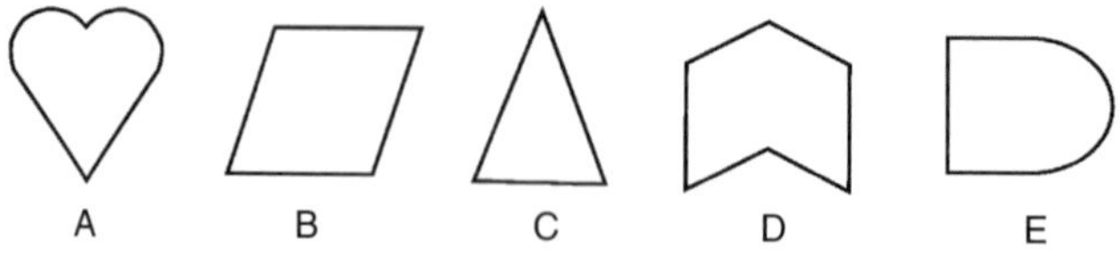

A B C D E

Answer ☐

Q26. (M2e,c) What is the missing number in the following series of numbers?
1, 2, 9, 64, 625, ?, 117 649.

    A. 1110
    B. 2048
    C. 6072
    D. 7776
    E. 8824

Answer [ ]

Q27. (M13d) The scatter graph compares the BMAT test results of 25 candidates in Tests 1 and 2.

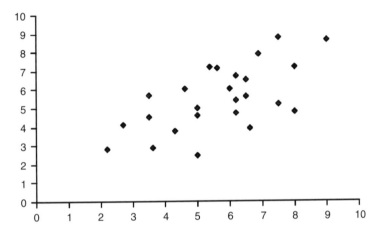

Which one of the following statements is true when comparing the test results in the two tests?

    A. There is a strong positive correlation.
    B. There is a weak negative correlation.
    C. There is a weak positive correlation.
    D. There is a strong negative correlation.
    E. There is no correlation negative or positive.

Answer [ ]

Q28. (M3,4) If Paul can paint a house in six hours and Julie can paint a house in nine hours, how long will it take them to paint a house if they both work together?

    A. 7 hours 30 minutes.
    B. 4 hours 32 minutes.
    C. 4 hours 24 minutes.
    D. 3 hours 45 minutes.
    E. 3 hours 36 minutes.

(hint: hourly rates)

Answer [ ]

Q29. (M2e) This is a code question. You have to break the code to work out the solution. If DICE = 3824 and DICE + FACE = 8848, then what number is represented by FACE – DACE?

    A. 5026
    B. 2000
    C. 6824
    D. 8500
    E. 1400

Answer [ ]

Q30. (A2, 3) The hypothesis that the earth's atmosphere is warming because of anthropogenic greenhouse gases is clearly true. Carbon dioxide emitted from power stations and car exhausts is the principal culprit. Methane, the second most important greenhouse gas, arises from the decomposition of organic matter on agricultural farms.

Which one of the following, if true, would seriously weaken the above argument?

    A. Climate change is a complex process and predicting it with any certainty is impossible in the short term.
    B. Carbon dioxide makes up less than 0.05 per cent of the earth's atmosphere so it cannot be responsible for global warming.
    C. Greenhouse gases released by human activities are not the primary source of greenhouse gases in the atmosphere.
    D. A thousand years ago atmospheric temperatures were higher than today and anthropogenic greenhouse gases were lower.
    E. Global warming did not begin until after the industrial revolution.

Answer [ ]

Q31. (A2, 3) Competitive sports should be removed from the school curriculum. Children who take part in sports and perform poorly may experience loss of self-esteem and feelings of inferiority in comparison with those who perform better.

Which of the following is an unstated assumption of the above argument?

A. Children are too young to take part in competitive sports.
B. Being very good at sport enhances self-esteem and leads to feelings of superiority.
C. Competition can be detrimental to psychological health.
D. It is not OK to try your best and fail.
E. Competitions create winners and losers.

Answer [ ]

Q32. (A2, 3) Medical school applicants can be split into two groups, A and B. Both groups achieve excellent A-level grades in the subjects with which they are familiar, but group A are better at solving the unfamiliar problems found in the BMAT. Group B can improve their BMAT scores with practice.

Statement: Intelligence is largely innate and relatively fixed, whereas 'thinking ability' can be developed.

Which of the following best describes how the short statement relates to the passage?

A. It has no relevance to the passage.
B. It presents a challenge to the passage.
C. It supports the passage.
D. It explains the poor performance of group B in the BMAT.
E. It neither supports nor undermines the passage.

Answer [ ]

Q33. (A2, 3) Chronic diseases are prevalent in the elderly population and 60 per cent of people attending GP surgeries with a chronic disease are aged 75 or above.

Which of the following is an implicit assumption of the above argument?

A. Sixty per cent of elderly people attend their GP.
B. Most elderly people attend their GP.
C. The over-75s attend the GP the most frequently.
D. Sixty per cent of elderly people have a chronic disease.
E. Few people attending their GP are under 75.

Answer [   ]

Q34. (A2, 3) Sodium fluoride should not be added to drinking water as it is poisonous at trace levels, especially for children. Toothpastes and mouthwashes contain the warnings 'do not swallow' and 'children should be supervised' as evidence of this. Whilst sodium fluoride was an inexpensive method of preventing dental carries in the past, better dietary habits, oral hygiene and the presence of fluoride in toothpastes now make the fluoridation of drinking water unnecessary.

Which one of the following, if true, would seriously weaken the above argument?

A. Some people cannot afford to buy toothpastes or fail to brush their teeth regularly.
B. There are no reports of fluoridated water having harmed a child.
C. The concentration of fluoride in drinking water is strictly controlled to be within safe limits.
D. The benefits in preventing dental carries are only small.
E. The safe limit for fluoride ion concentration is an arbitrary figure.

Answer [   ]

Q35. (A2, 3) Place the following four sentences in the order in which they form the most coherent passage.

   A. This produces a metal that is harder, more durable and easier to cast than copper.

   B. Thus, the earliest classification for system for tool making refers to a Stone Age, a Bronze Age and an Iron Age, with the very brief Copper Age omitted.

   C. The Bronze Age ended when metallurgists found how to extract iron from its ore and forge it.

   D. When humans first started making metal tools they used copper, followed soon afterwards by bronze, which is copper alloyed with tin.

Answer [   ]

Section 2 Scientific knowledge and applications

Mock test 8

27 questions
Time allowed 30 minutes
No calculators

Q1. (C4a) What is the percentage of hydrogen in water, atomic mass 18? Give your answer to one decimal place.

(hint: one mole)

Answer ☐

Q2. (P4c) From a standing start, a Boeing 747 takes off in 40 seconds. If the speed at the point of lift-off is 80 m s^{-1}, what is the average acceleration?

A. 2 m s^{-1}
B. 80 m s^{-2}
C. 20 m s^{-2}
D. 2 m s^{-2}
E. 40 m s^{-1}

(hint: units)

Answer ☐

Q3. (B2) Identify the correct path for food passing through the digestive system.

A. Pharynx, oesophagus, stomach, small intestine, large intestine.
B. Larynx, pharynx, oesophagus, stomach, duodenum, colon.
C. Pharynx, oesophagus, stomach, large intestine, small intestine.
D. Larynx, oesophagus, stomach, small intestine, large intestine.
E. Pharynx, oesophagus, stomach, ileum, duodenum, colon.

Answer ☐

Q4.   (C3a) Which one of the following describes correctly the chemical behaviour of fluorine?

A.   High electron affinity and a strong reducing agent.
B.   Most electronegative element and readily oxidized.
C.   Most electropositive element and readily reduced.
D.   Most non-metallic element and readily oxidized.
E.   High electron affinity and a strong oxidizing agent.

Answer [   ]

Q5.   (P18c,d, 17d) In the circuit shown below, what is the value of the current I?

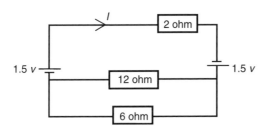

A.   2 A
B.   0.5 A
C.   1 A
D.   0.4 A
E.   3 A

(hint: parallel first)

Answer [   ]

Q6.   (M4a, 5) Calculate $\dfrac{5 + \dfrac{3}{8}}{2 - \dfrac{3}{4}}$

A.   3.6
B.   4.0
C.   4.3
D.   4.4
E.   4.8

Answer [   ]

Q7. (C4a) Quantitative analysis of a 5 g sample of an unknown compound showed that it contained 2 g of copper. Which of the following could be its chemical formula? (Atomic mass: $Cu = 64$, $C = 12$, $O = 16$, $S = 32$.)

A. CuO
B. Cu_2O
C. $CuCO_3$
D. $CuSO_4$
E. Cu_2SO_4

(hint: percentage)

Answer [ ]

Q8. (P10e) In a crown green bowling match, a bowl of mass $3M$ strikes a jack of mass M head on.

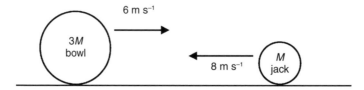

Before the collision the bowl has a velocity of 6 m s⁻¹ to the east and the jack has a velocity of 8 m s⁻¹ to the west. If the velocity of the bowl after the collision is 1 m s⁻¹ west, what is the velocity of the jack? Assume that the collision is perfectly elastic.

A. 13 m s⁻¹ east.
B. 13 m s⁻¹ west.
C. 14 m s⁻¹ east.
D. 14 m s⁻¹ west.

(hint: relative velocity; rebound)

Answer [ ]

Q9. (B2) Look at the list (1 to 6) below and then choose the correct path for carbon dioxide leaving the body during exhalation.

1 trachea; 2 bronchioles; 3 bronchi; 4 larynx; 5 pharynx; 6 alveoli.

A. 5, 4, 1, 3, 2, 6
B. 6, 2, 3, 1, 5, 4
C. 6, 2, 3, 1, 4, 5
D. 6, 2, 3, 4, 1, 5
E. 6, 3, 2, 1, 4, 5

Answer

Q10. (M2c, 6c) Calculate the following, giving your answer in scientific notation.

$$\frac{[32 + \log_{10}(10^8)]}{[8 \times 10^{-7} \times (10^3)^4]}$$

Answer

Q11. (P18a,b) Three resistors are connected to a power supply.

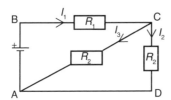

Which of the following statements are true and which are false, according to Kirchhoff's laws?

A. $I_1 = I_2 + I_3$

(hint: node C)

B. $V - I_1 R_1 - I_3 R_3 = 0$

(hint: loop)

C. $V - I_1 R_1 + I_2 R_2 = 0$

(hint: Kirchhoff?)

D. $V - I_1 R_1 - I_2 R_2 - I_3 R_3 = 0$

(hint loop?)

A. = ...
B. = ...
C. = ...
D. = ...

Q12. (C6a) A mouthwash contains 0.2% w/w sodium fluoride. What is the concentration of the fluoride ion in parts per million (ppm) if sodium fluoride is 45% fluoride ion by weight? (Per cent w/w = g /100 g water; ppm = g/million g water.)

A. 45 ppm
B. 450 ppm
C. 90 ppm
D. 900 ppm

Answer [　　　]

Q13. (B8(1)) If brown eyes (B) are dominant and blue eyes (b) are recessive, what is the probability that a child will inherit blue eyes if it has a heterozygous mother and a father who has homozygous brown- and blue-eyed parents?

A. 25 per cent
B. 33.3 per cent
C. 50 per cent
D. 75 per cent
E. 100 per cent

(hint: i) father; ii) Punnett square father/mother)

Answer [　　　]

Q14. (C5i, 6a,b) Choose the correct word or term (labelled A to K) from the list below to match each numbered space (i to v) in the following text. Some words or terms may be used more than once or not at all.

A = acid; B = base; C = salt; D = 0; E = turns litmus red; F = 7; G = compound; H = 12; I = ion; J = turns litmus blue; K = 13.

Sodium hydroxide is a strong [...i...]. A 0.01 molar solution has a pH of [...ii...] and [...iii...]. If 100 ml of the solution is titrated against 25 ml of 0.02 molar sulphuric acid the products are a [...iv...] and water; the final pH is [...v...].

i = ...
ii = ...
iii =......
iv =......
v = ...

Q15. (P17a,b) The diagram shows the position of two positively charged points, 1C and 2C (ie 2 × C) in a grid. In which square does the electric field have the greatest magnitude?

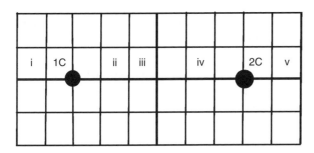

A. i
B. ii
C. iii
D. iv
E. v

(hint: inverse square; vectors)

Answer

Q16. (B8(2)) A mother expressing an X-linked dominant disease (A) and a father not expressing the disease have one affected son, one unaffected son and one unaffected daughter. Which of the following statements is true?

A. The father is X^AY
B. The mother is X^aX^a
C. The father is X^aY
D. The father is X^aY^A
E. No child is homozygous

(hint: female/male Punnett square; X^A male?)

Answer

Q17. (C10c) Choose the correct word or term (labelled A to J) from the list below to match each numbered space (i to v) in the following text. Some words or terms may be used more than once or not at all.

A = freezing; B = longest; C = evaporation; D = hydrocarbon; E = condensing; F = volatile; G = least; H = most; I = smallest; J = distillation.

In fractional [...i...] crude oil is separated into fractions. The [...ii...] molecules rise the highest up the tower before [...iii...]. The [...iv...] molecules are the [...v...] flammable and have the lowest boiling point.

i = ...
i = ...
ii = ...
iii = ...
iv = ...
v = ...

Q18. (P19d) The transformer shown below has an output rated at 240 volts and 7.5 amperes. What voltage and current are required at the primary coil?

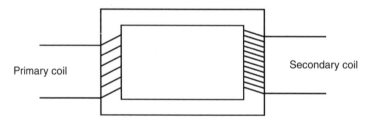

Primary coil

Secondary coil

A. 60 V, 15 A
B. 120 V, 30 A
C. 240 V, 15 A
D. 120 V, 15A
E. 360 V, 50A

(hint: power)

Answer ☐

Q19. (M11) If $y = 0$ when $x = 2$ or -2, what is the value of y when $x = 0$?

    A. +4
    B. –4
    C. +2
    D. –2
    E. 0

(hint: two brackets)

Answer ☐

Q20. (C7iii) The pH of blood is maintained at 7.4 by the carbonic acid hydrogen carbonate ion buffer as follows:

$$CO_2 + H_2O = H^+ + HCO_3^-.$$

What is the normal response to an increase in carbon dioxide levels in the blood?

    A. The equilibrium shifts to the right and the pH rises.
    B. The equilibrium shifts to the right and the pH falls.
    C. The equilibrium shifts to the right and the pH is unchanged.
    D. The equilibrium shifts to the left and the pH rises.

Answer ☐

Q21. (B6) Identify the substances i, ii and iii corresponding with the dominant transport processes for molecules passing through the nephron of a normal kidney.

	Transport process		
	Filtration	Re-absorption	Secretion
i	YES	NO	YES
ii	NO	NO	NO
iii	YES	YES	NO

    A. i = glucose; ii = creatinine; iii = protein.
    B. i = creatinine; ii = protein; iii = urea.
    C. i = protein; ii = salt; iii = glucose.
    D. i = creatinine; ii = protein; iii = glucose.
    E. i = urea; ii = protein; iii = creatinine.

Answer ☐

Q22. (M9a, e) The area of circle A is 16 times that of circle B, which is nine times that of circle C. If the diameter of circle A is 6 cm, what is the diameter of circle C?

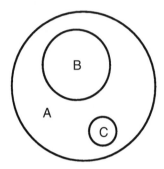

A. 0.25 cm
B. 0.5 cm
C. 0.75 cm
D. 1.0 cm
E. 1.2 cm

Answer ⬚

Q23. (B7). Two haploid gametes fertilize to give a diploid zygote that replicates by mitosis to give two identical daughter cells. How many copies of each chromosome are present in a daughter cell when the cells separate at the end of mitosis?

A. 0
B. 1
C. 2
D. 4
E. 8

Answer ⬚

Q24. (C9) The apparatus below shows the electrolysis of a dilute solution of sulphuric acid using carbon (inert) electrodes.

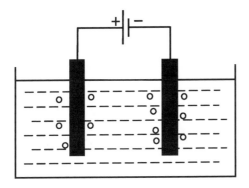

Choose the correct word or term (labelled A to H) from the list below to match each numbered space (i to v) in the following text. Some words may be used more than once or not at all.

A = hydrogen sulphide; B = decreases; C = remains the same; D = oxygen; E = twice; F = hydrogen; G = increases; H = half.

The gas discharged at the anode is [...i...] and the gas discharged at the cathode is [...ii...]. The volume of gas at the anode is [...iii...] the volume of gas at the cathode. The pH of the solution [...iv...] and the concentration of the solution [...v...] as the electrolysis progresses.

i = ...
ii = ...
iii = ...
iv = ...
v = ...

Q25. (P17d) The charge (Q) in coulombs stored by a capacitor C is given by the formula $Q = CV$ where C is in farads and V in volts. How long will it take to charge a 0.1 F capacitor with a 12 V power supply and a 100 mA charging current?

A. 0.12 s
B. 1.2 s
C. 12 s
D. 120 s
E. 1200 s

(hint: amps: charge s^{-1})

Answer [   ]

Q26. (M10, 11) If $y^2(x^2 - 2x + 1) = 9x^2 + 6x + 1$, what is y in terms of x?

    A. $y = 9x^2 + 6x + 1$
    B. $y = x^2 + 3x + 1$
    C. $y = (3x + 1)(3x - 1)$
    D. $y = (3x + 1)/(x - 1)$
    E. $y = (3x + 1)/x$

Answer

Q27. (C9, P14a, P15) The graph shows the time–temperature curve of a liquid when cooled at atmospheric pressure.

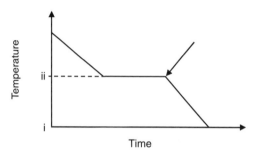

Which of the following statements are true and which are false?

Answer

A. Two phase changes take place.
B. The temperature remains constant during solidification.
C. All the liquid has solidified at the point shown by the arrow.
D. Adding impurities to the liquid will increase ii.
E. The melting and freezing points are the same.

Section 3 Writing task

Mock test 9

Choose one question
Time allowed 30 minutes; you have one side of A4 paper
No dictionaries

1. Not everything that can be counted counts and not everything that counts can be counted (Albert Einstein)

What do you think the author is implying by this statement? Write a unified essay, giving examples that explore the validity of the statement or otherwise.

2. The art of medicine consists in amusing the patient while nature cures the disease (Voltaire, 1694–1778)

What does the author mean by this statement and does it have any relevance today? Advance an argument that reconciles the art of medicine, as you see it, with ability of nature to cure disease.

3. Education is what remains after one has forgotten what was learned in school (Albert Einstein)

What do you understand by the above statement? Develop an argument that both advances the statement and refutes it?

Answers and explanations

ANSWERS TO REVIEW QUESTIONS

Answers to aptitude review questions: Argument

1. **Answer:** C (C offers an alternative explanation to the (false) premise that nuclear reactors are sited away from population centres on safety grounds).
2. **Answer:** A (A significantly weakens the argument on the basis that carbon is taken up (carbon cycle) and the carbon footprint is reduced; D and B are irrelevant because bio-diesel remains an alternative in reducing carbon dioxide emission; C lends support to the argument).
3. **Answers:** A and D (A and D challenge the premises of the argument; B, C and D, even if true, are outside the scope of the argument).
4. **Answers:** B and D (B is the same *method* if beetroot juice is a diuretic and D indicates that the data are valid only for non-hypertensive people; A, C and E may be true but they are irrelevant distracters).
5. **Answer:** B (The key word in the statement is '*but*' because it supports the argument (old bulbs phased out) with the proviso that wind turbines are needed (diversity in modern technologies).
6. **Answers:** C, A, D, B.

Answers to maths review questions

1. **Answer:** D ($1 - 0.25\pi$; circle $= (\pi \times 2 \times 2)/4 = \pi$; square $= 4$; area of four corners $= 4 - \pi$, so area of one corner $= 1 - 0.25\pi$).
2. **Answer:** E (50 cm^2; $AB^2 + AD^2 = 10^2$, ie $2AB^2 = 100$; $AB^2 = 50 =$ area).
3. **Answer:** B ($\sqrt{3}(x^2/4)$; split into two triangles of base length $x/2$, height h, so area ABC $= 2 \times$ (half base $\times$ height) $= 2(0.5 \times (x/2) \times h) = xh/2$, where h is found from

the Pythagoras theorem, ie $x^2 = (x/2)^2 + h^2$; so: $h^2 = x^2 - (x/2)^2$, from which it can be shown that $h = \sqrt{(4x^2/4 - x^2/4)} = \sqrt{3}x/2$. Finally, substitute this value of h into the area expression (area $= xh/2$) to give $x\sqrt{3}x/4$).

4. **Answer:** A (Pythagoras theorem: $h^2 = (4 - \sqrt{2})^2 + (2 + \sqrt{2})^2$, ie $h^2 = (16 - 8\sqrt{2} + 2) + (4 + 4\sqrt{2} + 2) = 24 - 4\sqrt{2} = 4(6 - \sqrt{2})$; take the square root to give $h = 2\sqrt{(6 - \sqrt{2})}$.

5. **Answer:** D (36 cm; area $= 3a \times 3a + 1/2 \times 4a \times 3a = 15a^2$; $15a^2 = 60$ so $a^2 = 4$ giving a $= 2$; perimeter $= 6 + 6 + 14 + CD$; $CD =$ hypotenuse h where $h^2 = 6^2 + 8^2 = 100$ so $h = 10$; $10 + 26$).

6. **Answer:** A (2π cm; $<ACB = 2 \times <ADB = 72°$ (using a circle theorem); $72°/360° = 1/5$; $1/5 \times \pi D = 1/5 \times \pi \times 10 = 2\pi$).

7. **Answer:** C (1.1296×10^4; $[6^{2/3}]^6 + [10^{4/5}]^5 = [6^{12/3}] + [10^{20/5}] = 6^4 + 10^4$. $= 36 \times 36 + 10000 = 1296 + 10000 = 11296$).

8. **Answer:** 1 (divide top and bottom by 3 and express in terms of 8^5:

$$\frac{3 \times (2^3)^5 - 2 \times 8^5}{1 \times 8^5} = \frac{3 \times (8)^5 - 2 \times 8^5}{1 \times 8^5} = 3 - 2 \div 1)$$

9. **Answer:** $x = 4/5$ (($5x - 2)^2 = 4$ so ($5x - 2) = \sqrt{4} = 2$; $5x = 4$).

10. **Answer:** D ($x = 3/2$; $(2x)^8 = (2x + 3)^4$ so $(2x)^2 = (2x + 3)^1$ then $4x^2 = 2x + 3$ and $4x^2 - 2x - 3 = 0$; $(2x + 1)(2x - 3) = 0$ so $2x = 3$ or $2x = -1$; $x = 3/2$ or $-1/2$).

11. **Answer:** 6 20p coins (let $x = $ 50p coins and $y = $ 20p coins, then: i) $x + y = 15$, $x = 15 - y$; ii) $50x + 20y = 570$, ie $5x + 2y = 57$ so $5(15 - y) + 2y = 57$; $75 - 5y + 2y = 57$; $3y = 18$; $y = 6$).

12. **Answer:** B ($5\tfrac{5}{7}$; i) $A^3 = 8B^3$ so $A = 2B$; $B = A/2$; ii) $C^3 = 1/8B^3$ so $C = B/2$; iii) box D $= 1000$ cm³; side length $= 10$ so $A + B + C = 10$; then $A + A/2 + (A/2)/2 = 10$; ie $4/4A + 2/4A + 1/4A = 7/4A = 10$ and $A = 40/7 = 5\tfrac{5}{7}$).

13. **Answer:** D ($x^2 - 16 = 0$; $(x + a)(x + b) = 0$; given that $a + b = 0$, then $a = -b$ and $ab = -16$ then $-a^2 = -16$ so $a = 4$ and $b = -4$ to give $(x + 4)(x - 4) = 0$ and finally $x^2 - 16 = 0$).

14. **Answer:** C (1st: $\dfrac{13}{52}$; 2nd: $\dfrac{12}{51}$; $\dfrac{13}{52} \times \dfrac{12}{51} = \dfrac{13}{13} \times \dfrac{3}{51} = \dfrac{1}{17}$).

15. **Answer:** D ($-4 \leq x \leq 1$; $x(2x + 6) \leq 8$; i) $\div 2$: gives $x(x + 3) \leq 4$; then ii) expand: $x^2 + 3x \leq 4$; iii) re-arrange: $x^2 + 3x - 4 \leq 0$; factorize: iv) $(x\ 1)(x\ 4)$, adding signs to give $(x - 1)(x + 4)$; finally sketch $y = x^2 + 3x - 4$, using the roots from the factored expression, ie when $y = 0$, $x = +1$ or -4 and when $x = 0$, $y = -4$.

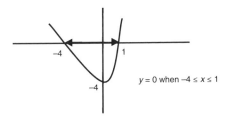

$y = 0$ when $-4 \leq x \leq 1$

16. **Answer:** A ($(ac - b)/(a - 1)$; i) cross-multiply: $(y - c) = y - b$; ii) expand: $ay - ac = y - b$; iii) collect y terms: $ay - y = ac - b$; iv) factorize and re-arrange to leave y on its own: $y(a - 1) = ac - b$ so $y = (ac - b)/(a - 1)$).

17. **Answer:** E (sin 270 = cos 180; these are both equal to − 1; the trough of the cosine wave is 90° behind the trough of the sine wave; the cosine wave peaks at +1 on the y-axis).

Answers to physics review questions

1. **Answer:** 1.25 m ($s = ut + 1/2\ at^2$; $a = g = 10$; $u = 0$; $h(s) = 5t^2 = 5 \times 0.25 = 1.25$).
2. **Answer:** 50 metres (2.5 seconds in flight; 2.5 s × 20 m s^{-1}).
3. **Answers:** A = gravitational force = 100 N; B = normal force = 100 N; C = friction force = 100 × 0.2 = 20 N; D = applied force = 20 N.
4. **Answer:** D: 10 m s^{-2} (B and C are speeds, not accelerations, so this leaves only A and D as possible answers. The acceleration due to gravity (g), which is 10 m s^{-2}, applies to all objects falling to earth, irrespective of their mass (and the speed at which they are thrown). The acceleration of the ball relative to the parachutist is also 10 m s^{-2} because he is not accelerating (terminal velocity reached; weightlessness), ie D).
5. **Answer:** 2.4 kW ((6000 kg × 10 N × 2 m) ÷ (50 s × 1000)).
6. **Answer:** 100 m s^{-1} ($PE_{lost} = KE_{gained}$, ie $mgh = 1/2\ mv^2$ which gives $v^2 = 2gh = 2 \times 10 \times 500 = 10\,000$ so $v = \sqrt{10\,000} = 100$).
7. **Answer:** 48 km (work done by scooter = $F \times d$ = 100 kg × 10 N × 10 per cent × d = 100d joules; work done by batteries: volts = joules per coulomb, ie joules = volts × coulombs = 24 × 2 × 10^5; hence 100d = 48 × 10^5 metres so d = 48 × 10^3 m = 48).
8. **Answer:** B (130 cm from $v = f\ \lambda$; or work with the units 260 Hz = 260 s^{-1} and v = 338 m s^{-1} so length (m) = 338 m s^{-1} ÷ 260 s^{-1} = 1.3 m).
9. **Answer:** 2 m s^{-1} (action and reaction are equal (Newton's third law) momentum of the bullet = momentum imparted to the gun (choose convenient units, both sides the same); 0.03 × 400 = 6 × V; V = 3 × 4 ÷ 6 = 2 m s^{-1}).
10. **Answer:** B (2.3 kW; $V = IR$ so 230 = I.23 giving I = 10 ohm; power = I^2R).
11. **Answer:** 540 kilojoules (3 kW = 3kJ s^{-1}; 3 kJ s^{-1} × (3 × 60 s) = 9 × 60 kJ).
12. **Answer:** D (J and L; H = uniform (constant) velocity; I = uniform (constant) acceleration; J = increasing velocity = *acceleration*; K = stationary; L = increasing velocity = *acceleration*; M = uniform (constant) velocity; H and M could also be a pair, as could I and L or I and J, but these are not answer choices).

Answers to chemistry review questions

1. **Answer:** B (atomic number = 14 protons = 14 electrons; atomic mass = protons + neutrons = 30; 30 − 14 = 16 neutrons; only the number of neutrons changes in isotopes).
2. **Answer:** C ($C_3H_6O_3$; divide by mass numbers 12, 1 and 16 to give 3:6:3).
3. **Answer:** C (2.4; 200 ml of 1.0 M HCl = 0.2 moles HCl, which consumes 0.1 moles of carbonate (leaving 0.4 moles unreacted), ie the acid is the limiting reactant).
4. **Answer:** a = 6, b = 6, c = 6 (ie all 6; carbons first: 6 CO_2 (b = 6); then hydrogens: 6 H_2O (c = 6); finally oxygen ('on its own'), we need 12 + 6 − 6 to balance the sides, ie 6 CO_2 (a = 6).

5. **Answer:** B (the oxidation states of H and F in forming the compounds are: H = +1, F = −1, and the sum of the oxidation states (oxidation numbers) equals zero for a neutral compound: CF_4 (+4), CH_4 (−4), C_2H_6 (−3), CF_3 (+3), C (0); the lowest of these is −4 in CH_4 (C is −4 and H is +1).

6. **Answer:** D (molecular mass NaCl = 23 + 35.5; so 9 g = 9 ÷ (23 + 35.5) moles NaCl; 1 mole NaCl contains 1 mole of Na).

7. **Answer:** C (there are four positive sodium ions on both sides of the equation which balance the negative charges, so the silver thiosulphate complex on the right-hand side carries no charge (Ag^0); so Ag^{+1} (as AgBr) is reduced to Ag^0, elemental silver, complexed).

8. **Answer:** E (lower the temperature to move the equilibrium to the right in an exothermic reaction and increase pressure because 3 moles become 2 moles. A catalyst increases the rate).

9. **Answer:** E (0.0001 M KOH: pOH = −$\log_{10}$ 0.0001 = 4 so pH = 14 − 4 = 10).

10. **Answer:** A, B, D, C (i = oxidation (A); ii = reduction (B); iii = O_2 (D); iv = Cu deposits (C)).

11. **Answer:** T, F, F, T, T (A = true; (3 phases (solid, liquid and gas) and 2 phase changes (solid to liquid; liquid to gas); B = false (temperature is below 273 K/0 °C; the freezing/melting point is at ii); C = false (boiling point is at iii); D = true (373 K = 100 °C); E = true (100 K rise from 0 °C to 100 °C)).

12. **Answer:** C, B, G, I, E (i = $C_{10}H_{22}$ (C); ii = C_8H_{18} (B); iii = C_2H_4 (G); iv = Br_2 (I); v = $C_2H_4Br_2$ (E)).

Answers to biology review questions

1. **Answer:** D (3:1; Punnett square: two Tt plants: TT, Tt, Tt = 3 tall; tt = 1 short).

2. **Answer:** B (Bb, bb; autosomal recessive; hence has to be bb to be affected).

3. **Answer:** A (AA, Aa, aa; autosomal dominant; hence AA or Aa = affected parent (male), aa = unaffected parent (female), Aa = affected child (daughter) and aa = unaffected child (son)).

4. **Answer:** E, G, J, K, F, D, H (i = autonomic (E); ii = rods and cones (G); iii = optic nerve (J); iv = efferent (K); v = ciliary (F); vi = distant (D); vii = convex (H)).

5. **Answer:** C (a surge in LH triggers ovulation, then progesterone rises to maintain the pregnancy).

6. **Answer:** D (most nutrients are absorbed in the small intestine; the pancreas releases enzymes to speed up the breakdown of food and an alkaline fluid to neutralize stomach acid).

7. **Answer:** B (3 genotypes: AA, Aa and aa, and 2 phenotypes (inherited traits), ie either homozygous/heterozygous dominant or homozygous recessive).

8. **Answer:** E (the pulmonary artery carries de-oxygenated blood to the lungs; ie less oxygen and more carbon dioxide than blood in the pulmonary vein).

9. **Answer:** C (large protein molecules and red blood cells are not filtered through the glomerular capillaries; NB: glucose is reabsorbed in the proximal tubule).

ANSWERS TO MOCK TESTS

Answers to Mock Test 1: Aptitude and skills

1. D	13. B	25. heart murmur
2. E	14. D	26. E
3. C	15. 8,13	27. C
4. 5/8	16. B	28. A and E
5. D	17. 43%	29. B
6. C	18. C	30. C
7. A	19. B	31. B
8. B	20. A	32. D
9. 2	21. D	33. 67
10. E	22. A	34. C
11. D	23. A and D	35. A
12. B, D, A, C	24. E	

1. **Answer:** D (D expresses the main thrust of the argument; A and B are not stated; C is true but misses the main point; E is false).
2. **Answer:** E (E neither supports or challenges the argument because the people it describes are also failing to maintain their health, but it does not say that they should be discriminated against).
3. **Answer:** C (only C challenges the main conclusion of the argument that nuclear power is both cheap and clean; A, B, D and E are concerned with individual premises).
4. **Answer:** 5/8 (square say $1 \times 1 = 1$; $ABC = 1/2 \times 1/2 \times 1/2 = 1/8$; $CDE = 1/2 \times 1 \times 1/2 = 1/4$; shaded $= 1 - 1/8 - 1/4 = 1 - 3/8$).
5. **Answer:** D (per 100 K = × 10 per million so UK boys + girls = $(3200 + 2000) \times 12 = 5200 \times 12 = 62\,400$).
6. **Answer:** C (UK boys = $3200 \times 12 = 38\,400$; Spain boys = $800 \times 10 = 8000$; difference $= 38\,400 - 8000 = 30\,400$).
7. **Answer:** A ($320{:}200 = 32{:}20 = 8{:}5$).
8. **Answer:** B (Spain has the highest boy:girl asthma admission ratio at 2:1).
9. **Answer:** 2 (the thick diagonal remains in a fixed position and the thin line moves a small amount to the right and downward).
10. **Answer:** E (not producing any power (the reason for the claim) makes a power source poor (the claim)).
11. **Answer:** D (D is the best answer because most of the tests are contaminated and therefore of no help to identifying antibiotic sensitivity; in A, waiting for the results is contraindicated if there a high proportion of false positives; B is not to be inferred because the restriction to one antibiotic is not stated; C should read a low proportion of true positives; E is false).
12. **Answers:** B, D, A, C.
13. **Answer:** B (B correctly identifies the assumption that finding a host is all that is required for pathogenic bacteria to cause an infection; A is false/not stated; C is true

but fails to validate the argument; D is a distractor that re-states the argument using 'high probability' in place of the certainly implied statement; E is stated).

14. **Answer:** D (the argument can only leap to its final conclusion by assuming that the medical profession supports the use of cannabis in MS, which is not the same as acknowledging that it can relieve symptoms. A, B and C are all stated in the premises and E is neither stated nor assumed).

15. **Answer:** 8, 13 (0, 1, 1, 2, 3, 5, 8, 13, 21, 34, 55 etc; the Fibonacci series, ie each new term is the sum of the two terms before it).

16. **Answer:** B (76; example method: visualize in three layers each 5 cm deep; top layer = 0 without icing; middle layer = $4 \times 4 = 16$ without icing (and 20 around the outside with icing); bottom layer = same as middle layer = 16. Total portions = $36 \times 3 = 108$; 108 less $16 + 16 = 76$).

17. **Answer:** 43% ($100 - 50 = 50$; $50 \times 1.4 = 70$; $70 \times \% = 100$ so $\% = 100 \div 70 = 10/7 = 142.9 = 142.9\%$, ie $+ 43\%$).

18. **Answer:** C (Speed–time graph: calculate all four *areas* (ie distances apart): HI = $0.5 \times 20 \times 40 = 400$; IJ = $0.5 \times 20 \times 30 = 300$; JK = $(0.5 \times 10 \times 30) + (10 \times 30) = 450$; KL = $0.5 \times 20 \times 30 = 300$).

19. **Answer:** B (15; draw a hexagon and join all the vertices).

20. **Answer:** A (1. School X = $800 \times 0.25 = 200$ A-grades and school Y = $660 \times 0.3 = 198$ A-grades, ie *true*; 2. C + B + A = $66\% \times 800 = 528$, ie *true*; 3. Y pass rate minus X pass rate = $72\% - 66\% = 6\%$, ie false; 1. and 2. only).

21. **Answer:** D (D is the best answer because it is contrary to the view that chocolate is preferred to healthier food on a cost per calorie basis; A misses the key point altogether; B is counter to the argument; C may be true but it is irrelevant).

22. **Answer:** A (A reflects autonomy, informed choices and the need for 'treatment based on what each individual believes'; B is refuted because the doctor can indicate the preferred option; C and D might be inferred but they do not reflect the passage as a whole).

23. **Answers:** A and D (if A and D are true then the argument is flawed because pensioners can draw on additional sources of income; B does not challenge the 15% of GPD statement and C works out to be no more than 12 per cent of GDP (4% + 8% max).

24. **Answer:** E (500 per cent increase = $\times 5$ (5-fold); angina = $9.1 \div 1.3$ (700%); MI = $1.7 \div 0.3 = 17 \div 3$ (500+ %); stroke = $1.8 \div 0.1 = 18 \times 10$ (1800%)).

25. **Answer:** heart murmur (variation = max. minus min. = $2.2 - 1.0 = 1.2$).

26. **Answer:** E (none; eg draw three circles that satisfy the description yet challenge the statements).

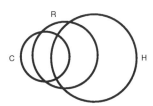

27. **Answer:** C (a true conclusion can be arrived at (accidentally) from false premises; eg replace *aptitude* (the word that links i) with ii)) with *entrance*).

28. **Answers:** A and E (answer A is clearly expressed in the last sentence; answer E must be true when comparing winter and summer deaths if the difference between winter and summer deaths is as stated in the second sentence. B cannot be inferred from the text; C is not the paradox, which is that mortality rates are higher in winter than in summer but not in colder countries compared with warmer countries; D is false because the increasing prosperity refers to warmer countries only).

29. **Answer:** B (B lends the greatest support to the argument because it links mental arithmetic ability with fewer errors; A attempts to undermine the argument; C offers limited support (with no link between over-confidence and errors); D re-states the meaning 'order of magnitude').

30. **Answer:** C (15; $550 - 400 = 150/10$ years = 15/yr).

31. **Answer:** B (20 million; reading from the graph: 500 per million in 1995; we have $10\,000$ giving $10\,000 \div 500 = 100 \div 5 = 20$).

32. **Answer:** D (Zak is older than Carl and Leanne is older than Carl so Carl cannot be the second oldest; example of continuum for young to old: Richard, Carl, Leanne, Sarah/Zak).

33. **Answer:** 67 ($T1 = 60 \times 0.5 + 72 \times 0.5 = 30 + 36 = 66$; $T2 = 90 \times 0.4 + 55 \times 0.6 = 36 + 33 = 69$; $T1 = 2/3$, and $T2 = 1/3$; $66 \times 2/3 + 69 \times 1/3 = 44 + 23 = 67$).

34. **Answer:** C (not A because McDonald's does not have the sole right to the prefix Mc; not B because a sign saying Norman McDonald is permissible; not D because it needs to be a food business; C correctly surmises that any attempt to benefit trade by association with the McDonald's chain is defamatory).

35. **Answer:** A (according to the passage any food business placing Mc in front of the name runs a high risk of being forced to change its name; three examples are given in the passage and answer A is consistent with them; answer C is incorrect because the passage indicates a name change with no mention of a fine).

Answers to Mock Test 2: Scientific knowledge and applications

1. **Answer:** A (atomic mass = protons + neutrons = 64; atomic number = the number of protons (defines the element) = 29 for Cu, with 29 electrons for a neutral atom and 27 electrons for a 2+ cation, ie protons + neutrons + electrons = 64 + 27 = 91).

2. **Answer:** 45 m (two methods: i) conservation of energy (best method): KE lost = PE gained: $1/2\ mv^2 = mgh$, ie $v^2/2 = gh$; $30 \times 30 \div 2 = gh$; $450 = 10h$ so $h = 45$ m.
   ii) equations of motion (alternative method): $v^2 = u^2 + 2gh$ with $v = 0$ at the highest point and $g = -10$ m s^{-2} ('deceleration'); $0 = 30 \times 30 + (2 \times -10 \times h)$; $20\ h = 900$ so $h = 45$ m.)

3. **Answer:** D (Right atrium, tricuspid valve, right ventricle, pulmonary artery (via pulmonary valve); 'tricuspid before bicuspid').

4. **Answer:** 9 moles ($2C_8H_{18} + 25O_2 = 16CO_2 + 18H_2O$; $18 \div 2 = 9$).

5. **Answer:** E (27 N; $4 \times 10 = 40$; $40 \times 4 = F \times 6$; $F = 2/3 \times 40 = 80/3 = 26.7$ N).

6. **Answer:** B (48 mph; C, 50 mph is wrong because the time intervals for the two journeys differ. Instead calculate the total time for the round trip and divide this into the total distance for the round trip, ie $240 \div (2 + 3) = 48$).

7. **Answer:** C (carbon forms covalent bonds).

8. **Answer:** D (3 pence; $13 \times 230 \div 1000 \times 4/60 \times 15 = 13 \times 0.23 = 2.3 + 0.69 = 3$).

9. **Answer:** C (chest muscles contract, chest expands, pressure falls, air inspired).

10. **Answer:** J, F, A, C, K, E (i = compound (J); ii = atoms (F); iii = element (A); iv = molecules (C); v = oxidized (K); vi = proton (E)).

11. **Answer:** B (lowest velocity = highest pressure).

12. **Answer:** 15 ($2.5 = (y + 1)^{0.25} + 0.5$; $2 = (y + 1)^{0.25}$ so $2^4 = (y + 1)$; $y = 16 - 1$).

13. **Answer:** C (the concentration of salt is highest at the bottom of the loop of Henle; the diagram indicates that only water leaves at 2, thus concentrating the salt, and that by 4 this concentration has reduced because only salt leaves).

14. **Answers:** C and D (carbon dioxide and hydrofluoric acid form acidic solutions).

15. **Answer:** 10 ohms ($2 + 3 + 5$).

16. **Answer:** E (0%; autosomal recessive inheritance pattern with neither parents of M having an affected dominant allele, ie heterozygous (Aa; Aa) and carriers of a recessive condition such that M must be homozygous recessive (aa) to be affected. His children cannot be affected unless his wife is affected or a carrier).

17. **Answer:** D (carbon monoxide and hydrocarbons are burnt in oxygen; oxygen is removed from nitrogen oxides).

18. **Answer:** D ($F = ma$ for all three couplings; we have $F_i = (20 + 15 + 10) \times 0.4$; $F_{ii} = (15 + 10) \times 0.4$; $F_{iii} = (10) \times 0.4$; ie 18, 10 and 4).

19. **Answer:** 8 £5 notes (let $a = £5$, $b = £10$ and $c = £20$, then $5a + 10b + 20c = 400$ (given) so i) $a + 2b + 4c = 80$; ii) $b = 2a$; $c = b - 6$ (given); substituting ii) in i) gives $a + 2(2a) + 4(2a - 6) = 80$ so $a + 4a + 8a - 24 = 80$ gives $13a = 104$; $a = 8$).

20. **Answers:** C and E (propene is an unsaturated hydrocarbon (C–C double bonds); it reacts with bromine and burns in air to produce carbon dioxide and water)).

21. **Answers:** C and D (eg at $Hb_{50\ per\ cent}$ the partial pressure of oxygen *increases* from approx 27 to 33; at $P_{50\ per\ cent}$ the saturation level drops approx 8% from 83 to 75).

22. **Answer:** D $(x - 3x - 10 \leq 0$; $(x + 2)(x - 5) = y$; $y = 0$ when $x = -2$ or 5 and when $x = 0$ $y = -10$; solution from graph: $-2 \leq x \leq 5$, ie the only possible values of x are $-2, -1, 0,$ 1, 2, 3, 4, 5).

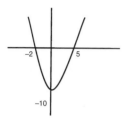

23. **Answer:** C, B, E, F (i = oxidation reaction, loss of electrons (C); ii = reduction reaction (B); iii = Cl_2 (E); iv = H_2 (F). Note that O_2 will form at the anode in a very dilute NaCl solution).

24. **Answer:** D (4, ie two double strands of DNA).

25. **Answer:** A (1.8×10^{18} hertz (Hz); $E = Fh$ so $1.2 \times 10^{-15} = F \times 6.63 \times 10^{-34}$. then $F = 1.2 \div 6.63 \times 10^{19} = 12 \div 6.63 \times 10^{18}$. No further working out is required; only A and E have the correct order of magnitude (10^{18}) and $12 \div 6.63$ must be less than 2 so the only possible answer is 1.8×10^{18} = A).

26. **Answer:** C ($3\frac{3}{4} : (25 + 1/8) \div (7 - 3/10) = 201/8 \div 67/10 = 201/8 \times 10/67 = 3/8 \times 10 =$ $30/8 = 3\frac{3}{4}$).

27. **Answer:** 880 kJ ($4.2 \times 1000 \times (100 - 0) = 420$ kJ to reach boiling point and a further $2.3 \times 200 = 460$ kJ to boil 200 g).

Answers to Mock Test 4: Aptitude and skills

1. A	13. B	25. E
2. B	14. A	26. C
3. C	15. B	27. B
4. D	16. C	28. D
5. 28%	17. D	29. D
6. E	18. D and E	30. E
7. C	19. E	31. B
8. S	20. C, B, D, A	32. C
9. C	21. D	33. B
10. D	22. A	34. A and B
11. E	23. C	35. B and E
12. B	24. D	

1. **Answer:** A (A is a hypothesis that makes sense and is probably true; B is too sweeping a hypothesis; C and D are hypotheses without any foundations and are probably untrue).

2. **Answer:** B (B takes for granted that locally produced food has a lower carbon footprint; A is stated and C, D and E are different arguments).

3. **Answer:** C (more vehicles is a valid alternative explanation for more congestion; A (true or not) is irrelevant as the argument makes no such correlation; B supports the argument; D has no link between economic activity and congestion).

4. **Answer:** D (speed–time graph: the greatest *acceleration*, negative or positive, is given by the steepest *slope*, ie J, and the least *displacement* is the least *area* under the interval, ie M; at I the speed is at its highest and constant so the acceleration is zero).

5. **Answer:** 28% ($100 - 20 = 80$; $80 - 8 = 72$; $100 - 72 = 28$).

6. **Answer:** E (E is correct in stating that there is a significant challenge to the argument if 90 per cent of crimes fail to reach court; only a small reduction in crime is anticipated by handing down longer sentences).

7. **Answer:** C (answer C rejects the conclusion that doctors are over-eager to prescribe antibiotics; A explains why doctors might over-prescribe but not why the conclusion is unsafe; B is irrelevant to the argument, and both D and E can be inferred from the argument, so none of these can be the correct answer).

8. **Answer:** S (I and X are easily eliminated because they look the same whether turned upside down or reflected in a mirror; B, C and E do not have rotational symmetry and when turned upside down the left becomes the right, which is then reversed back again on reflection when the right becomes the left, so not B, C or E. S has rotational symmetry and appears unchanged on turning upside down and is thus incorrect after reflection).

9. **Answer:** C (A = 1, B = 2, C = 3, D = 4 etc; every column/row adds to up 12).

10. **Answer:** D (two bars have similar heights and two bars have very different heights so not B; A and C are the same so neither of these; ie D pie chart (shortest bar = smallest segment and longest bar = largest segment)).

11. **Answer:** E (2030; *slow method*: you can calculate the gradient from two convenient points (eg 1970 and 1987.5) to see that the line rises by 10 percentage points every 17.5 years; then from 1970 (a convenient point) the line needs to rise exactly 35 percentage points to reach the one-car line; ie $(35 \div 10) \times 17.5$ years = 61.25, $+1970 = 2031.25$; *quick method* (approx.): in the 30 years between 1970 and 2000 the line has risen half the distance it needs (approx 17 per cent) to reach the one-car line and will take another 30 years to hit it if trends continue).

12. **Answer:** B (2/5, ie (initial – final)/initial = $(50 - 30)/50$); NOT $20\% = 1/5$).

13. **Answer:** B (400% increase; (final – initial)/initial $\times 100\% = (1/2 - 1/10) \div 1/10 \times 100\% = 4/10 \times 10 \times 100\% = 400\%$).

14. **Answer:** A (A is an unwarranted assumption because the argument offers no explanation for what it claims other than to state that it is common sense; B is true and cannot be an assumption; C is an implicit assumption of the argument if it is to hold true; D overstates anything that is presumed; E can be discounted on the basis that it refers to the occupants rather than just the driver).

15. **Answer:** B (B is the best answer because it makes no additional assumptions and appears to be the most probable; A and D might be true but there is no evidence given to substantiate these claims; C goes too far in what it claims).

16. **Answer:** C (correlation mistaken for causation (no proven link); only C offers an alternative explanation, ie diagnosis is linked with child's age).

17. **Answer:** D (A is entirely erroneous; B is true as far as it goes; C could be true but is unsubstantiated; E is false because low incomes are a basis for defining poverty; D is the best answer because it acknowledges that few people are living in absolute poverty, with relative poverty and social exclusion described in terms of unequal resources).

18. **Answers:** D and E (D offers an alternative explanation and E contradicts the argument; B neither contradicts nor offers an alternative; both A and C support the argument).

19. **Answer:** E (3.9 and below = 1/4, so 4.0 and above = 3/4; 6.9 and below = 3/4, so 7.0 and above 1/4; 3/4 × 1/4 = 3/16).

20. **Answers:** C, B, D, A.

21. **Answer:** A (Z has lowest proportion without SEN; you need to compare the without/with ratios to find the proportions. V = 700:250 (2.8); W = 250:100 (2.5); X = 400:150 (2.7); Y = 200:50 (4); Z = 600:300 (2). Note that Y has the highest proportion without SEN but the lowest number.

22. **Answer:** A (65 per cent; 'decipher' the question and break it down; the total SEN (Z, Y, X, W, V) = 300 + 50 + 150 + 100 + 250 = 850; the two schools with highest number (not proportion) are Z and V = 300 + 250 = 550; % = 550/850 × 100% = 55/85 × 100 = 11/17 × 100 = 1100/17 = 64.7%).

23. **Answer:** C (4 per cent; step i) SEN with FSM = 850 × 40% = 340; step ii) without SEN with FSM = 426 − 340 = 86; step iii) without SEN = 600 + 200 + 400 + 250 + 700 = 2150; step iv) 86/2150 × 100% = 43/1075 × 100% = 4300/1075 = 4%).

24. **Answer:** D (7; $(12 − n) + n + (11 − n) = 18$; so $23 − n = 18$ giving $n = 5$, and then Chemistry only $12 − n = 7$).

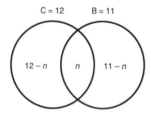

C = 12   B = 11

12 − n   n   11 − n

25. **Answer:** E (2.0 L; add x litres of 1.0 molar solution to 0.5 litres of 6.0 molar solution to give $(0.5 + x)$ litres of 2.0 molar solution; total moles of saline are unchanged so write: $1.0x + 0.5 \times 6 = 2.0(0.5 + x)$, giving $x + 3 = 1 + 2x$; $x = 2$).

26. **Answer:** C (thiazide diuretic: according to Table 2 the next treatment option would be Step 2, ie add a calcium channel blocker (C) to the ACE inhibitor (A) to give A + C. However, according to Table 1, calcium channel blockers (C) are contraindicated in heart failure. This leaves only the diuretics 'thiazide' and 'furosemide' as answer choices (beta-blockers (B) are not a treatment option in patients with diabetes); finally, thiazide is selected before furosemide according to Table 2).

27. **Answer:** B (calcium channel blocker (CCB): according to Table 2, adding a CCB would be the next treatment option; class B is indicated for angina but not for asthma and is not a treatment option for patients with diabetes).

28. **Answer:** D (29: first round = 32 – 2 = 30 players = 14 matches + 2 unmatched players (automatic win); second round = 8 matches (16 players); third round = 4 matches; fourth round = 2 matches; fifth round final = 1 match. The total number of matches = 14 + 8 + 4 + 2 + 1 = 29).
29. **Answer:** D (£1.05; $t + m = 1.10$; $t – m = 1.00$; so $2t + 0 = 2.10$, then $t = 1.05$).
30. **Answer:** E ($\pi/6$: sphere: $(4\pi/3)r^3$; cube: $(2r)^3 = 8r^3$; ratio = $(4\pi/3)/8 = \pi/6$).
31. **Answer:** B (B offers an alternative means by which smokers would generate tax revenues if they stopped smoking; A is true but does not link tax and the economy; C is true but introduces new arguments; D is true but is not part of the conclusion).
32. **Answer:** C (C is the only statement that must be false; that patients can make a prior expression of a refusal to treatment should an emergency situation arise is clearly stated so it cannot be ignored).
33. **Answer:** B (08.50 hrs; Phoebe: $d = st = 3t$; then for Zak: $d = 12(t –15/60)$; distance d is the same when they meet, so $3t = 12(t – 1/4)$, giving $9t = 3$, ie $t = 1/3$ hr = 20 mins; adding this to Phoebe's time gives 08.50 hrs).
34. **Answers:** A and B (A is easily inferred from the fact that disulfiram is indicated to be an *adjunct* therapy; B is more difficult to infer, though the paragraph clearly states that alcohol dependency means that the abuser is unable to stop drinking under any circumstances, making disulfiram therapy entirely inappropriate).
35. **Answers:** B and E (A is incorrect because alcohol abuse is indicated to lead to dependency in some people but not others; C is incorrect because it is alcohol dependency that is the disease process; D is the exact opposite of that stated).

Answers to Mock Test 5: Scientific knowledge and applications

1. **Answer:** 3 moles ($3 \times 2 \times 0.5$ moles, per mole of compound).
2. **Answer:** B 1.28×10^6 (the table shows that the activity reduces fourfold every day, ie by 2×2 (two-half lives per day); $32 \times 10^4 \times 2 \times 2 = 1.28 \times 10^6 = $ B).
3. **Answer:** C (left atrium, bicuspid (mitral) valve, left ventricle, aorta).
4. **Answer:** E (the oxidation states of H, C and F in forming the compounds are: H = +1, C = +4, F = –1, and the sum of the oxidation states (numbers) equal zero for a neutral compound: H_2O (–2), O_2 (zero), H_2O_2 (–1), CO_2 (–2), OF_2 (+2); the highest of these is +2 in OF_2 (O is +2 and F is –1)).
5. **Answer:** 230 N (change in momentum ÷ time taken; $0.046 \times 50 \div 0.01 = 230$).
6. **Answer:** B 2.25π (square = 3×3 so circle diameter = 3, then area of circle = $\pi D^2/4 = \pi \times 9/4 = 2.25\pi$).
7. **Answer:** C (atomic number = 36 protons = 36 electrons; atomic mass = protons + neutrons = 83.8; 83.8 – 36 = 47.8 neutrons, and 0.8 neutron is not possible, so there must be isotopes with different numbers of neutrons).
8. **Answer:** 3 amps (look carefully to see that the battery is across *both* the 2 ohm bulb and the 4 ohm resistor, ie they are wired in parallel. However, you are not asked to calculate the overall resistance so you do not need to use the reciprocal law: 6 volts across a 2 ohm bulb draws 3 amps from $V = IR$; (and 6 volts across a 4 ohm resistor draws 1.5

amps). Check: total current drawn = 4.5 amps and total resistance is given by $1/R_{tot}$ = 1/2 + 1/4 = 3/4; R_{tot} = 4/3; $V = IR$ so V = 4.5 × 4/3 = 1.5 × 4 = 6 v (ie checks correct).

9. **Answers:** J, G, C, H, A, E, I, A, D (i = thyroid (J); ii = endocrine (G); iii = metabolism (C); iv = hormones (H); v = pituitary (A); vi = hypothalamus (E); vii = cold (I); viii = pituitary (A); ix = more (D)).

10. **Answers:** B and E (only the alkenes (C_nH_{2n}) are unsaturated and react with bromine by addition).

11. **Answer:** C (Ali: 300 kg m (3000 J) and 15 kg m s^{-1} (150 W).

12. **Answer:** B 5.67 × 10^{12} (write all three as 10^{12} ie 5.2 × 10^{12}, + 0.48 × 10^{12} – 0.01 × 10^{12} = (5.2 + 0.48 – 0.01) × 10^{12} = 5.67 × 10^{12}).

13. **Answer:** 5500 Pa (or 5.5 kPa; volume = 20 cm × 10 cm × 5 cm = 1000 cm^3; 1000 cm^3 × 11 g cm^{-3} = 11 000 g = 11 kg; 11 kg × 10 N kg^{-1} = 110 N (force).
Area = 20 cm × 10 cm = 200 cm^2 = 0.02 m^2. Pressure = force ÷ area = 110 ÷ 0.02 = 110 × 50 = 5500 Pa).

14. **Answer:** A (ultrafiltration (Bowman's capsule), active transport (selective re-absorption), osmosis (water), active transport (salt), osmosis (water)).

15. **Answer:** A (acidosis: excess CO_2 leads to the accumulation of hydrogen ions with a drop in pH).

16. **Answer:** C, B, E, F (i = oxidation reaction (C) with iii (E) chlorine released); ii = reduction reaction (B) with iv (F) hydrogen released).

17. **Answer:** B (method: determine whether abnormality is dominant or recessive (ie not A, autosomal dominant, because neither of the parents can possess an affected dominant gene); B autosomal recessive is possible with both parents carrying the recessive gene (ie heterozygous carriers for the disease); not X-linked because males are not carriers of X-linked conditions).

18. **Answers:** A = gravitational force = 120 N; B = normal force = gravitational force = 120 N; C = applied force = friction force = 30 N; D = net force = 0 (constant velocity = no acceleration).

19. **Answer:** D ($x^2(4 – \pi)/4$; square – circle = $x^2 – \pi x^2)/4$ = $(4x^2 – \pi x^2)/4$ then factorize to give $x^2(4 – \pi)/4$; NOT answer C, which expands to give $x^2/4 – \pi x^2/4$).

20. **Answers:** B, E, D, B, H (i = boiling points (B); ii = hydrocarbon (E); iii = volatile (D); iv = boiling points (B); v = top (H)).

21. **Answer:** E (receptor, afferent/sensory neurone, central nervous system, efferent/ motor neurone, effector/muscle).

22. **Answer:** A ($16\pi^2r$ newtons; $F = ma = 4 \times v^2/r$ where v = distance ÷ time (ie circum- ference ÷ time for one revolution) = $2\pi r \div 1 = 2\pi r$ so $v^2/r = (2\pi r^2)/r = 4\pi^2 r$ and F is then given by $4 \times 4\pi r^2 = 16\pi r^2$).

23. **Answer:** B 5/6 (four face cards have been removed to leave 48 cards and eight face cards. The probability of drawing a face card is now 8/48 = 1/6 and the probability of NOT drawing a face card is 1 – 1/6 = 5/6. NB: the question does not ask what is the probability of drawing the four face cards in sequence).

24. **Answers:** A, C, E, H, B, G (i = gene (A); ii = chromosome (C); iii = allele (E); iv = zygote (H); v = genotype (B); vi = phenotype (G)).

25. **Answer:** A (nitric oxide is a compound, not a mixture).

26. **Answer:** C ($x\sqrt{3}$; drawn a diagonal on the base to give two triangles at right angles, ie a base triangle and a second triangle that includes the diagonal line you want. Pythagoras: base diagonal squared = $x^2 + x^2 = 2x^2$; cube diagonal squared = $2x^2 + x^2 = 3x^2$ so cube diagonal = $x\sqrt{3}$).

27. **Answers:** F, F, T, T, T (A = false; 2 phases (liquid, solid) and one phase change between them (liquid to solid); B = false (could be any temperature below 373 K/ 100 °C; C = true (boiling point reached); D = true; E = true (pressure lower, boiling point lower)).

Answers to Mock Test 7: Aptitude and skills

1. B	13. C	25. B
2. 56%	14. D	26. D
3. E	15. E	27. C
4. B and D	16. A	28. E
5. D	17. B	29. A
6. E	18. C and D	30. D
7. A	19. E	31. C
8. A	20. C	32. C
9. B	21. D	33. B
10. C	22. B	34. B
11. B	23. E	35. D, A, C, B
12. C	24. 3 litres	

1. **Answer:** B (acceleration–time graph: acceleration × time, ie *area* under the interval = *change in velocity;* H and I look the strongest candidates; I = rectangle = 15 × 30 = 450 and H = rectangle + triangle = (20 × 10) + (0.5 × 20 × 20) = 400); hence I).

2. **Answer:** 56 per cent (100 × 1.8 = 180; 100 ÷ 180 = 10/18 = 5/9 = 0.5555 = 55.55 per cent).

3. **Answer:** E (E is the best answer because it is an alternative to the suggested treatment).

4. **Answers:** B and D (B weakens the ethical position of the argument by offering strong ethical reasons in opposition; D weakens the 'nothing position' assumed of placebo treatments; A fails to challenge the argument and C lends support to it).

5. **Answer:** D: ('cause and effect' not proven; a sedentary lifestyle also leads to a weight increase through increased food intake, ie correlation but no causation).

6. **Answer:** E 1/4 (visualize shapes in turn: small square = 1/4 (2/8); rectangle (half the small square) = 1/8; large triangle = 1/4 (2/8); small triangle (half the large triangle) = 1/8; 1 – 6/8 = 1/4).

7. **Answer:** A (Norton, Ningwood and Niton).

8. **Answer:** A 4.3 per cent (P++ (true+) = $0.005 \times 0.9 = 0.0045$; P– + (false+) = $0.995 \times 0.1 = 0.0995$; total positives = $0.0045 + 0.0995 = 0.104$ of which 0.0045 are true, ie percentage is given by $(0.0045 \div 0.104) \times 100\% = 45 \div 1040 \times 100\% = 9 \div 208 \times 100\% = 900 \div 208 = 4.3\%$).

9. **Answer:** B 28 per cent (estimate bar lengths in (unspecified) units: males $2 + 2 + 2 + 4 = 10$; females = $1 + 1 + 4 + 8 = 14$; difference = $14 - 10 = 4$; $4/14 = 28/98 = 28$ per cent (approx) fewer males than female (check: 14×72 per cent = 10); note conversely that there were 40 per cent more female deaths than male: 10×140 per cent = 14); 'than female' means use female as the starting point).

10. **Answer:** C (add male and female bar lengths by eye and compare ratio of the totals; ie under 65s = 3 divisions (2 male + 1 female); similarly 65–74 total approx 3 divisions (so answers C, D or E), in which case over 85 = 4 male + 8 female = 12 = C only). Put simply, if under 65 = 3, then over 85 = 12).

11. **Answer:** B 8300 (total bar units = 24 (add all bar lengths or tally column C); bar length for females over 85 = 8 units (7.9) = 1/3 of all deaths = approx 8333. Put simply, the female over-85 bar is one-third of the total lengths).

12. **Answer:** C (52 million; $25\,000 = 0.048$ per cent so 100 per cent = $25\,000 \div 0.048 \times 100$ per cent = 25 million $\div 0.48$ giving 2500 million $\div 48 = 52$ million).

13. **Answer:** C (answer C correctly summarizes the key point of grey power, ie more older voters acting in their own interests).

14. **Answer:** D (D is the best answer because it indicates that there could be *alternative* explanations for aggressive behaviour, so reducing screen violence may not be the *best* way to reduce real-life violence).

15. **Answer:** E (not joining a gym (the reason for the claim) makes us less interested in keeping fit; A and D are too firm and too specific; B and C are distracters that are barely hinted at).

16. **Answer:** A (the paragraph indicates that the *concentration* of PSA in obese men is lower whereas the statement indicates that the *total amount* of PSA in obese men is higher, which at first appears contradictory (answer B). However, the concentration could be lower even if the total were higher, so the statement fails to support or challenge the argument, ie A).

17. **Answer:** B (26 bands: $(0.5)^x = 1{:}60$ million (given); $(1/2)^x = 1/60 \times 10^6$ and $(1/2)^x = 1/2^x$ (because $1^x = 1$) so $1/2^x = 1/60 \times 10^6$; thus $2^x = 60 \times 10^6$; solve, eg $2^5 = 32$ so $2^{10} = 32 \times 32 = 1024$ and $2^{20} = 1024 \times 1024$, ie >1 million; $2^{25} > 32$ million; $2^{26} > 64$ million).

18. **Answers:** C and D (A is true (end of whisker); B is true ($6.4 - 3.8 = 2.6 =$ interquartile range); C is false (lower quartile = 3.8 marks or less); D is false (*median* mark was 5.2); E is true (upper quartile = 6.4 so three-quarters achieved this mark or below, ie 1/4 achieved more than 6.4; the probability of two students achieving more than 6.4 = $1/4 \times 1/4 = 1/16 = 6.25\%$).

19. **Answer:** E (step i): one sector is half the size of the other, which occurs in columns A, C and E but not B and D (ruled out); step ii) C is not possible because no two sectors are the same, so this leaves A and E; step iii) A is 1/8, 1/4, 1/2 (too big), so not A, which leaves E (1/8 (80), 1/4 (160), 280 (7/16), ie fits).

20. **Answer:** C (2006; children's books (CH) accounted for the smallest *proportion* (fraction) in 2006, whereas adult special interest accounted for the smallest proportion in the other years; 2002 CH is a distracter, ie NOT A).

21. **Answer:** D (57%; greatest diff. = highest − lowest; ie 2002 to 2006: 35 to 55; % increase = $(55 − 35)/35 \times 100\% = 20/35 \times 100\% = 4/7 \times 100 = 400/7 = 57\%$).

22. **Answer:** B (£60 000; 2002 to 2004; estimate £65 000 to £125 000; no other answer is close).

23. **Answer:** E (9; draw a table after noting that 1/4 are fiction and 3/4 non-fiction; 24 are paperbacks and 12 are hardbacks).

	P	H	
F	6	3	1/4
N	18	9	3/4
	24	12	

24. **Answer:** 3 litres (1 drop/3 s = 20 dp/min = $20 \times 0.1 = 2$ ml/min = 120 ml/hr = 120 ml/hr × 25 hr = 0.12 litres × 25 = $12 \times 0.25 = 3$ litres).

25. **Answer:** B (a rhombus has two lines of symmetry; the remaining shapes all have one line of symmetry).

26. **Answer:** D (7776; $1^0 = 1$; $2^1 = 2$; $3^2 = 9$; $4^3 = 64$; $5^4 = 625$; $6^5 = 7776$ etc).

27. **Answer:** C (there is a weak positive correlation; the points are not sufficiently close to a straight line for it to be a strong correlation; positive because as one test result increases so does the other).

28. **Answer:** E (3 hours 36 minutes; Paul one-sixth per hour; Julie one-ninth per hour, so together = $1/6 + 1/9 = 3/18 + 2/18 = 5/18$ per hour, ie 18/5 hr = 3 3/5 hr).

29. **Answer:** B (2000; code: A = 0, B = 1, C = 2, D = 3, E = 4, F = 5, G = 6 etc; DACE = 3024).

30. **Answer:** D (D challenges the hypothesis because it states that atmospheric temperatures have been higher than they are today without anthropogenic greenhouse gases).

31. **Answer:** C (C correctly identifies the unstated assumption (the link) that it is the competing (not just the taking part) that can be psychologically damaging; B re-states the argument from the opposite perspective; A, D and E can be excluded on the basis that they introduce new arguments).

32. **Answer:** C (both groups do well at A level (innate intelligence) and group B's ability to think through unfamiliar problems (thinking ability) can be developed (improved scores) with practice; not D because a poor performance is not indicated in the paragraph).

33. **Answer:** B (for the argument to hold true, most (prevalent) of the elderly population must attend their GP; if only a small proportion visit their GP (eg 10%) the argument is false).

34. **Answer:** B (B seriously undermines the argument if there is no evidence of harm done).

35. **Answer:** D, A, C, B.

Answers to Mock Test 8: Scientific knowledge and applications

1. **Answer:** 11.1% ($2(H) \div 18(H_2O) = 1 \div 9 = 0.111 = 11.1\%$).
2. **Answer:** D (2 m s^{-2}; m s$^{-1} \div$ s $=$ m s^{-2}; 80 m s$^{-1} \div 40$ s $= 2$ m s^{-2}).
3. **Answer:** A (pharynx, oesophagus, stomach, small intestine, large intestine).
4. **Answer:** E (high electron affinity (strong acceptor of electrons, forming F$^-$; the most electronegative element); strongly oxidizing (more than O$_2$) and therefore readily reduced (oxidation number decreases 0 to -1); most non-metallic element).
5. **Answer:** B (0.5 amp; $1/R_{parallel} = 1/6 + 1/12 = 3/12$; $R_{parallel} = 12/3 = 4$; then $R_{series} = 4 + 2 = 6$, and $V = IR$ so $I = V/R = 3/6 = 0.5$).
6. **Answer:** C ($43/8 \div 5/4 = 43/8 \times 4/5 = 43/2 \times 5 = 43/10 = 4.3$).
7. **Answer:** D ($2g/5g = 40\%$; $64/(64 + 32 + 4 \times 16) = 64/160 = 4/10$).
8. **Answer:** A (13 m s^{-1} east; i) the relative velocity method only works for elastic collisions: $v_1 - v_2 = u_2 - u_1$ taking care to include the negative sign in front of velocities to the west (right to left): $u_2 - u_1 = -8 - (6) = -14$ so $v_1 - v_2 = -14$; and $v_1 = -1$ (given), ie $v_2 = -1 + 14 = +13$ m s^{-1}; ii) conservation of momentum method applies to all collisions: $m_1u_1 + m_2u_2 = m_1v_1 + m_2v_2$ so $3M \times 6 + M(-8) = 3Mv_1 + Mv_2$; $18 (-8) = 3v_1 + v_2$ (cancelling M's) so $3v_1 + v_2 = 10$; $v_1 = -1$ (given), which gives $v_2 = 10 -(-3) = +13$ m s^{-1} as in i); iii) kinetic energy is conserved in perfectly elastic collisions so: $(m_1u_1^2 + m_2u_2^2) = (m_1v_1^2 + m_2v_2^2)$ (cancelling the 1/2 both sides), noting that energy is a scalar ($\pm v$ squared is always positive), so: $3M(36) + M(64) = 3M(1^2) + M(13^2)$, ie $108 + 64 = 3 + 169$; $172 = 172$ (ie elastic).
9. **Answer:** C (expire via: alveoli, bronchioles, bronchi, trachea, larynx, pharynx).

10. **Answer:** 5.0×10^{-5} $((32 + 8) \div (8 \times 10^5) = 40 \div (8 \times 10^5) = 5 \times 10^{-5})$.

11. **A: true** (at node C); **B: true** (for loop ABCA); **C: false** (for loop ABCDA; $-I_2R_2$); **D: false** (not a loop).
12. **Answer:** D (900 ppm; 0.2% w/w = 0.2 g/100 g = 2000 g/million g, ie 2000 ppm; $2000 \times 45\% = 900$ ppm).
13. **Answer:** A (25 per cent; father's parents are homozygous brown (BB) and homozygous blue (bb) so he has a Bb phenotype (heterozygous); mother is stated to be heterozygous (Bb). A Punnett square for Bb father and Bb mother shows that bb (homozygous blue) = 25 per cent chance (1 in 4) with three genotypes (BB, Bb and bb).

	B	b
B	BB	Bb
b	Bb	bb

14. **Answers:** B, H, J, C, F (i = base (B); ii = $14 - 2 = 12$ (H); iii = turns litmus blue (J); iv = salt (C); v = 7 (F)).

15. **Answer:** E (v; electric field lines (vectors) radiate outwards from both positive charges; the magnitude is greatest near to the stronger 2C charge and reduces between the charges because like charges repel).

16. **Answer:** C (the father is X^aY; A can be ruled out (dominant A = expressed) as can B (no dominant a = not expressed); D can be ruled out (Y linked); this leaves C and E. Try a Punnett square for X^AY and X^AX^a; unaffected daughter homozygous).

	X^A	X^a
X^a	X^AX^a	X^aX^a
Y	YX^A	YX^a

17. **Answers:** J, I, E, B, G (i = distillation (J); ii = smallest molecules (I); iii = condensing (E); iv = largest molecules (B); v = least flammable (G)).

18. **Answer:** D (120 V, 15 amps; power in (VI watts) = power out (if 100% efficient) = 1800 W, so only answers D and E are possible; secondary coil has ×2 more windings than primary coil so voltage stepped up (×2) not down, ie 240 V).

19. **Answer:** B (–4; $(x – 2)(x + 2) = y$ satisfies $y = 0$ when $x = 2$ or –2; so when $x = 0$, $y = –2 \times 2 = –4$).

20. **Answer:** C (increased CO_2 shifts the equilibrium to the right and the *buffer* maintains the pH at 7.4).

21. **Answer:** D (ii must be protein because this is the only substance not to be filtered out, ie leaves choices B, D and E; iii useful substances are re-absorbed, ie glucose in C or D, hence D).

22. **Answer:** B (0.5 cm; A = 16B, B = 9C so A = 16 × 9C = 144C, ie area C = area A/144 and diameter C = diameter A/$\sqrt{144}$ = diameter A/12 = 6/12 = 0.5; the diameter of a circle is proportional to the square root of its area).

23. **Answer:** A (there are four copies at the start of mitosis (in prophase), ie two copies from each parent, but there are *no* copies immediately the cells separate).

24. **Answers:** D, F, H, B, G (i = oxygen (D); ii = hydrogen (F); iii = half (H), $H_2O = H_2 +0.5O_2$); iv = decreases (B); v = increase (G)).

25. **Answer:** C (12 s; $Q = CV = 0.1 \times 12 = 1.2$ coulombs = 1.2 amp for 1 second or 1 amp for 1.2 seconds; we have 100 mA (0.1 amps), hence takes 12 seconds).

26. **Answer:** D ($y^2(x^2 – 2x + 1) = y^2(x – 1)(x – 1)$ and $9x^2 + 6x + 1 = (3x + 1)^2$; taking the square root of both sides gives $y(x – 1) = 3x + 1$ so $y = (3x + 1)/(x – 1)$).

27. **Answers:** F, T, T, F, T (A = false; only 1 phase change (liquid to solid); B = true (remains at temperature ii until complete); C = true (fully solidified then cools); D = false (impurities depress the freezing point, eg antifreeze); E = true ('opposite directions' but occur at the same temperature)).

With over 42 years of publishing, more than 80 million people have succeeded in business with thanks to **Kogan Page**

www.koganpage.com